No levels available 3/17

CHRISTOPHER
COLUMBUS

HOW HE DID IT

Charlotte and David Yue

Houghton Mifflin Company
Boston   1992

Library of Congress Cataloging-in-Publication Data

Yue, Charlotte.
  Christopher Columbus: How He Did It / by Charlotte and David
Yue.
    p. cm.
  Summary: Detailed description of Columbus's voyage to the New
World in 1492.
  ISBN 0-395-52100-9
    1. Columbus, Christopher—Juvenile literature.   2. America—
Discovery and exploration—Spanish—Juvenile literature.
3. Geography—15th–16th centuries—Juvenile literature.
[1. America—Discovery and exploration—Spanish. 2. Columbus,
Christopher.] I. Yue, David. II. Title.
E118.Y84 1992   91-19624
917.04'15—dc20   CIP
                      AC

Printed in the United States of America

HAL 10 9 8 7 6 5 4 3 2 1

To Dony Sony

Contents

CHRISTOPHER
COLUMBUS

The Great Enterprise

In the dark of the Palos harbor, three small ships stood gently swinging at anchor. The sails were tightly furled and the ships almost seemed to be sleeping as they rocked in the waters. It was not yet dawn on Friday, August 3, 1492. Already it was oppressively hot and there was not a breath of wind.

Half an hour before sunrise, the captain of the fleet, a man with white hair, intense blue eyes, and a ruddy complexion, gave the orders to get under way. Suddenly the stillness was broken and the ships came to life with commotion and activity. Commands echoed from deck to deck and sailors chanted as they loosed the moorings, the lines that held the ship at dock, and weighed anchor. Men heaved and strained and the windlasses creaked as the anchor ropes were hauled on board. The admiral's banner, a dark green cross on a white background, was hoisted on the flagship. But the flag was motionless; there was no wind. The sails were limp and still.

Although all the men on board would have liked the blessing of the wind as they began this voyage, lack of wind would not stop them. The time of their departure had been chosen to take advantage of the tides. As the tide ebbed back toward the sea, the small fleet began to move very slowly down the river of Saltés. Friends and relatives who had come to see them off waved and shouted their farewells. The sailors manned the sweeps, using the oars to guide the ship down the river.

That particular day of departure had been chosen because of other events taking place in Spain at that time. The King and Queen had ordered all Jews to become Christians or leave the country. Thousands of people were forced to give up their homes and all they owned. All ships transporting these refugees had to leave port on August 2, 1492. Departure date was set for the following day. Even so, one ship of the tragic migration dropped down the river of Saltés on the same tide with the small fleet.

At last the three ships and the ninety men aboard them were alone in the Ocean Sea. They were beginning a journey that would change the course of history and extend the boundaries of the known world.

The captain of this fleet was Christopher Columbus

— sailor, merchant, mapmaker, and navigator of distant seas. He had left his birthplace of Genoa, Italy, many years before. In the course of his travels, he had been shipwrecked in Portugal. The Portuguese were expert seamen, and he learned many things about ships and sailing from Portuguese navigators. Columbus never went to school, but he taught himself several languages, read a great deal, made careful observations, and thought deeply. He formed a plan that came to be known as the Great Enterprise. The basic idea was simple enough. Since the world was round, it should be possible to reach the rich trading lands of the East by sailing westward.

This was a bold and dangerous plan. Columbus would have to sail into uncharted parts of the earth. No

one knew for certain how great the distance was between the known lands of the West and the mysterious lands of the East. No one knew what bodies of land might lie in the vast, unmapped ocean or what dangers would have to be faced along the way. Members of the crew may have had doubts and fears as they ventured out to explore the unknown, but Columbus was certain this enterprise was possible and that he would reach the East by this route.

Explorers, when they set sail, usually had some destination in mind. Sometimes, like Columbus, they believed they could find a new route to a known place. Sometimes they believed they could find a place they had read about or had heard of from other sailors.

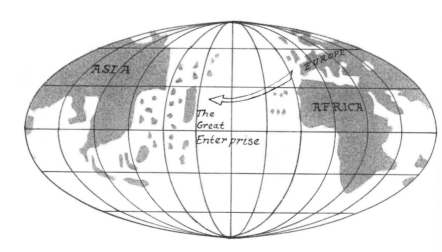

Columbus's Conception of the Earth

Other explorers extended the limits of the known world by traveling a charted route and sailing a bit farther, as did the men who explored the coast of Africa. Discoveries were rarely the result of random wandering but of a carefully planned search.

Chance and luck played a part in all discovery. Navigators sometimes came upon unknown lands that they had not expected to find. Sometimes they found open sea where they had expected to find land. Winds, currents, and storms could pull a ship off its intended course and prevent the would-be discoverer from reaching his destination or lead him to a great discovery he never imagined. But a discovery could benefit other people only if it could be charted and found again. After being tossed around by the sea, a sailor might not have a clear idea of where his discovery lay. The land he found might be forgotten or added to the many legends told in medieval Europe. Many discoveries were made by men who were searching for something quite different from what they found.

Successful explorers never have more than the minimum amount of equipment and information. Not only do they fight the elements, but they must compete against others who strive for the same goal. If explorers wait too long and are too cautious, they find the footprints of bolder adventurers when they finally reach their destination. The first person to cross the boundary of the known world must risk much to win glory.

It had taken Columbus many years of struggles and

disappointments to reach that day in 1492. Although he often must have felt quite alone in his belief in this plan, it was something he could not accomplish alone. The technology of the time needed to be developed enough so that he could have reliable ships and a means of finding the way. Other people had to risk their lives and their money on this project. Responsible rulers and careful investors would not send ships on long and dangerous voyages into the unknown merely in the hope of making chance discoveries, or to investigate vague reports of discoveries made in the past. Columbus had to convince powerful people and their committees of experts that he had strong evidence that his plan was reasonable and had a good chance of success. He had to convince them that the venture would be profitable. Explorers usually had high hopes that their efforts would bring fame and fortune to themselves and to their supporters at home.

Columbus never doubted that his Great Enterprise would succeed. He had a map and a plan. He was confident that he knew exactly where he was going. He intended to sail straight across the ocean until he reached the other side. There he expected to find Japan, China, and India. He had made his calculations of how far he had to travel and felt certain that they were correct. He believed his ships could go far enough and hold enough drinking water and supplies for the journey. He felt certain he had the tools and skills to find his way. And he had faith that God would guide and help him. If he lacked anything, he would make up for it by determination and skill. As Columbus looked out across the sea five hundred years ago, he was leaving all the disputes and refusals behind. The sea was his realm, and he believed the fulfillment of his dreams was within his grasp.

The Motives

There were many good reasons not to sail off to explore uncharted parts of the world. People always fear the unknown, and at that time the sea held even more mysteries than it does today. Sailors spent their lives at the mercy of its forces, and they wanted to keep to safe routes to known places where they stood a good chance of making a profit.

One of the greatest fears of fifteenth-century seamen was sailing into unknown waters and being unable to return. They had good reason to be afraid. At first the ships most commonly used had only one mast and one square sail. They were difficult to handle and depended on having a favorable wind. If the prevailing currents and winds carried the ship in one direction, it might be perilous, if not impossible, to sail in the opposite direction to get back again.

Even if the navigator could find winds and currents that could take the ship there and back, the unknown waters often hid deadly reefs, rocks, and shallows. Finding places to get fresh water was always crucial to survival on long sea voyages. The ship might safely reach land only to be met by hostile inhabitants. Terrifying legends and superstitions about the sea and the dangers it held were common. Sailors heard stories of boiling seas, temperatures so hot that no European could survive, and gigantic sea monsters that could smash any ship and devour its crew. Many thought the risks were not worth taking.

Yet by 1492 exploration had become so important to people and governments that they were willing to take enormous risks, and any knowledge they could gather about unknown lands and routes was carefully guarded. Portugal had an official policy of secrecy so that other countries would not find out any information about land discovered for Portugal. World charts were watched over like precious jewels. A special office was in charge of the production, revision, and filing of maps and charts. Navigators were issued these charts for each voyage but had to give them back when they returned. Anyone found taking maps out of the country without permission was subject to the death penalty.

Why had exploration become so important? Trade with the East was essential to European peoples and their way of life. Spices, which came from the East, were a necessary part of cooking. There was no refrigeration, and salting and smoking were the only ways of preserving food for storage. Food was often scarce. Spicy sauces disguised the taste of meat and fish that had begun to decay and relieved the monotony of eating the same kind of food day after day. Pepper was highly prized in the Middle Ages. It had a strong taste, and people believed that it helped them digest their food. Many of the spices used in cooking were also used as medicines. These spices were grown only in the Indies — lands of the Far East including what is now India, China, Indonesia, and Japan. Goods changed hands many times before reaching Europe, and all the people involved in this profitable trade tried to keep secret exactly where and how the spices were grown.

Silks, jewels, and other luxuries that Europeans wanted also came from the Indies. Anyone who was successful at transporting these goods to Europe could become very rich. Entire cities had become wealthy and important from trading. Trade with the East, however, was extremely difficult. The journey took months or even years. Caravans had to travel across barren deserts and steep mountains. Traders had to endure hunger and thirst, baking heat and freezing cold. Disease and accidents were frequent dangers. Murderers and thieves were constant threats. Places that would provide temporary shelter and food charged high prices. Ships could carry cargoes over the parts of the journey that

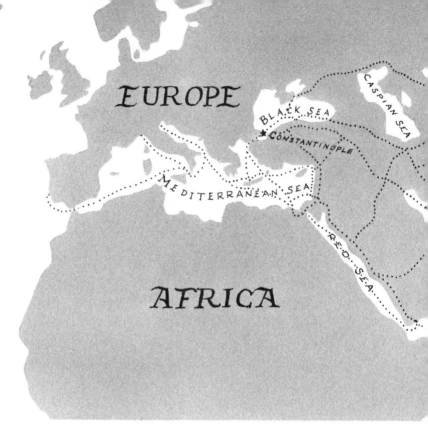

could be made by sea, but the sea routes were also dangerous and full of delays. All these difficulties made goods from the East enormously expensive.

Still, it was a profitable business. A large quantity of valuable cargo could be carried in one shipment. To try to understand the value and importance of spices, consider some later voyages that did reach the East. In 1497 when Vasco da Gama reached India by sailing around Africa, he brought back a cargo of pepper, cinnamon, ginger, and precious stones. The whole journey took two years, and two-thirds of the crew died, but the sale of the cargo was worth sixty times the cost of the expe-

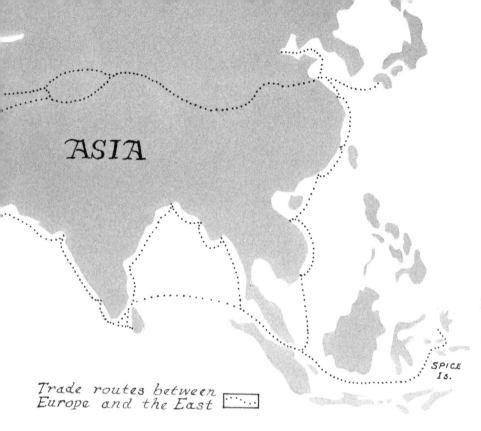

ASIA

SPICE
Is.

Trade routes between
Europe and the East

dition. When Magellan set sail for the Spice Islands in 1519, he had a fleet of five ships and a crew of 234 men. The voyage was expected to take two years. It took three years. Only one ship made it back, Magellan had been killed, and only eighteen men survived. But they managed to bring a cargo of cloves and cinnamon in the one remaining ship. The spices paid for all the ships and wages and still left a fantastic profit. For the backers, it had been a very successful voyage.

Finding a safer, easier route to the Far East had been an important concern for a long time. In 1453, when Columbus was two years old, something happened that made trade with the East even more difficult and costly. The city of Constantinople fell to the Muslim ruler Muhammad II. Constantinople had been a stronghold of Christianity and a major crossroads for trade. Christians and Muslims had been enemies for centuries. Now this road was blocked, and ships were no longer allowed into the Black Sea. The effects were soon felt by European merchants and seamen. Finding a new route to the East took on a greater urgency. And any country that could successfully find the way would have great political and economic power.

Learning about the unknown became more important. Many people thought there might be a longer but easier sea route. One idea was to sail around Africa to the Spice Islands. Little was known about Africa, so no one knew how far south a ship would have to sail or what dangers the men would encounter.

In Portugal, Prince Henry the Navigator was one of the first to realize the importance of exploration. He set up a base for sending out ships and collecting information. He employed the best chart makers, astronomers, and master mariners of his day. He made sure that the voyages were well planned and well equipped. He listened patiently to all stories of successes and failures, and noted and cross-checked all information. New discoveries were added to the charts, and these charts were available to future explorers.

For a long time, seamen believed that no ship ever returned from Cape Bojador in Africa. There was good reason for sailors to be afraid. A strong current and prevailing winds push constantly to the south. There are dangerous shallows and frequent storms. Prince Henry encouraged the development of ships that could be handled more easily in all weather conditions and even when sailing into the wind. Gil Eanes rounded Cape Bojador in 1434. The fears and darkness that overshadowed the continent of Africa and the Atlantic Ocean were gradually being pushed back. Step by step, explorers made progress and added new pieces to the known world.

Successful explorers gained in importance and fame. In the fifteenth century that was a strong motivation for taking risks. People lived in clearly marked social classes. The kinds of clothing, behavior, and food per-

Madeira 1418

Cape Bojador 1434
Cape Blanco 1441
Cape Verde Is. 1444

Cape Verde 1445

AFRICA

Fernando Poo 1475

Congo River 1482

Cape Cross 1486

Cape of Good Hope 1488

Portuguese Exploration of African Coast

mitted from class to class were sometimes even regulated by law. Opportunities to move up the social scale were rare. Columbus had a contract with the King and Queen of Spain that listed the titles and privileges he and his descendants would have if he succeeded. When Columbus's son became a viceroy, his wife received the unusual honor of being allowed to have gold and jewels on the saddle and trappings of her horses.

Columbus also believed he had a duty to bring Christianity to any lands he discovered. Queen Isabella of Spain also saw this as an important reason for exploration. When Columbus promised that his enterprise would lead to the expansion of Christianity, the Queen listened more favorably to his adventurous idea. Columbus was a sincere and dedicated Christian. At that time many Christians believed it was part of their mission to convert people to their religion. Many also thought it gave them a right to conquer other lands to make Christians of the people living there.

There were stories of great Christian leaders in Asia who had not had contact with Christians of the West for centuries. The tales of Prester John, in particular, excited the interest and imagination of Europeans for centuries. Prester John was a legendary priest-king, a rich and mighty ruler of a Christian kingdom believed to be somewhere in Asia or Africa. Hopes of finding Prester John or other powerful Christians were other motives for traveling to the East. Many Europeans hoped that such a leader would attack the Muslims from the east while Europe launched a new crusade from the west. The world in which Columbus grew up was threatened by conflicts with Muslims and the advance of Islam into Europe. Every voyage of exploration held the possibility of finding allies in the crusade against the Muslims. Rulers in Europe also hoped to learn more about the strength of the enemy. News and knowledge of the East were scarce and spread slowly. Explorers might be able to bring back information about how powerful and widespread Muslim rule actually was in Asia and Africa.

Columbus was setting out to accomplish great things. He was determined that on this journey he would spread the Christian faith, contact possible allies, add to the knowledge of the world, bring glory to Spain, and gain wealth and honor for himself and his supporters.

Evidence and Clues

CHAPTER THREE

Getting the Facts

Columbus set out certain about what he was going to accomplish and sure that he had the ability to succeed. What evidence did he have? What course of reasoning brought him to these conclusions? Columbus found out as much as he could about the known world and its size. He made his calculation of the size of the earth. He worked out the probable distance he would have to travel across the Atlantic to reach Asia. He learned all he could about the winds and currents. A scientist studying the problem of navigating the Atlantic under the conditions that faced Columbus in 1492 would have made the same kind of investigations and gathered the same information as Columbus did.

In the fifteenth century, Western civilization was centered on the Mediterranean Sea. The wintry Scandinavian lands, Iceland, Greenland, and the islands of Britain were the northern limits of the known world. The groups of recently discovered islands in the Atlantic — the Canary Islands, the Azores, Porto Santo, and Madeira — were at the western horizon of oceanic ventures. To the south were the deserts of North Africa, with the Portuguese rapidly filling in the African coastline.

To the east was Asia. Medieval Europeans knew little about it. Crusaders and traders brought back scraps of information, and myth and legend filled in the rest. Much of the East was not geographical territory to Europeans. It was more a fairyland of fabulous wealth. One-eyed monsters, people with one immense foot that they used as a sunshade, mermaids, and other marvelous creatures had appeared as facts in geographies and travel books for centuries.

Columbus gathered information about the known world in his travels as a sailor. He had been to England and Iceland from December 1476 to the spring of 1477. There he could have heard tales of mysterious lands lying to the west across the ocean. He might have heard stories of lands that the Vikings found west of Greenland, but if so, he did not realize the significance of these voyages. These lands, if considered at all, were viewed as legends or simply as other outlying islands of Europe. They were not believed to be parts of Asia or identified as part of a new continent. Columbus probably heard tales of Saint Brendan's venturing into the great sea and finding an island that many thought was the promised land of the saints. On many maps, Saint Brendan's Island appeared at different places in the Atlantic Ocean.

Columbus married the daughter of the first governor of Porto Santo around 1479, and over the next several years they lived on both Porto Santo and Madeira. During this time he made many trading voyages in the Canaries and the Azores. In the Azores Columbus heard of some strange events that he found very interesting. People showed him huge reeds and strange plants not grown anywhere in Europe or Africa that had been cast onto the shores of the islands. Another time, the sea brought the bodies of two men of a strange race. Boats and curiously carved pieces of wood had also washed ashore. These things were usually found after the wind had blown from the west for many days. Columbus guessed that they came from Japan or islands near it. He concluded that Japan was within reasonable sailing distance. He also made careful note that there were winds blowing from the west and an easterly drift of ocean currents in the latitude of the Azores.

Columbus also found out as much as possible from books. The invention of printing with movable type was one of the greatest events in the history of Western culture. Printing had long been used in China, but it was unknown in Europe until the middle of the fifteenth century. Europe was awakening from the Dark Ages; people were ready to accept new ideas. The printing press made books and information available to vast numbers of people. Many classical writings were also being rediscovered, translated, and printed. The Gutenberg Bible was printed just a year after the fall of Constantinople. Just as Europeans were learning more about faraway countries from books, these countries were becoming more difficult to reach and information about them was harder to get.

Some of Columbus's books still exist with the notes he wrote in the margins. Columbus owned a copy of Marco Polo's *Description of the World*. Marco Polo was a merchant's son who was in the East from 1273 to 1292. He became an official in the service of Kublai Khan, the grand ruler of China at that time. His book, one of the greatest travel books of all time, was published in many languages and widely read. Marco Polo wrote about the rich and powerful island kingdom of Cipango, now known as Japan, located in the sea to the east of Cathay, or China. Most of the information Europeans had about Japan came from Marco Polo. He described Cipango as an island rich in jewels, with temples and palaces of gold. Columbus's imagination was stirred by these vivid tales, and his geographic ideas were shaped by Marco Polo's information. But Marco Polo's geography was not always very accurate. He overestimated the size of Asia and the distance by sea from China to Japan. This strengthened Columbus's belief that the distance between Europe and Japan was not large and that Japan could be reached by sail.

Another important book Columbus read was Ptolemy's *Geography*. Ptolemy was a Greek scholar who lived in the second century. His work was rediscovered and made available in print. Ptolemy's book contained good advice about how scientific research should be conducted, a section of maps, and rules for scientific mapmaking.

In the Middle Ages, maps showed more about the spiritual beliefs of the times than about the size and shape of the earth. A circular diagram was often drawn showing the three known continents, with Jerusalem at the center. These maps were frequently beautiful works of art decorated with ornaments and drawings. But you could not estimate the distance between Rome and Jerusalem by measuring the map.

Back in the second century, Ptolemy figured out a method for locating places on a grid of intersecting lines of latitude and longitude. When Ptolemy's work was rediscovered in the middle of the fifteenth century, this came as a new idea. People now began to think of maps

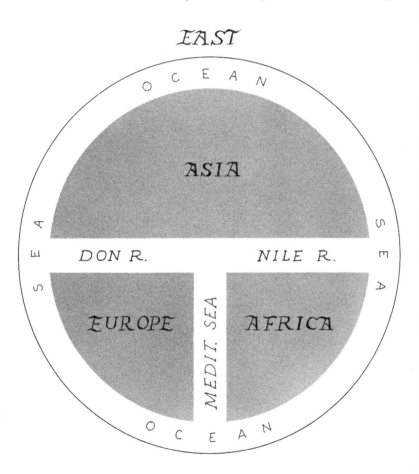

Circular Diagram of the Known World

*Circular Map Showing a Spiritual View
of the World*

as accurate representations of the earth. They wanted a
picture of the world that would show the relative size
and shape of the countries. People thought more about
the size of the world. They wondered how much of the
earth was land and how much was sea.

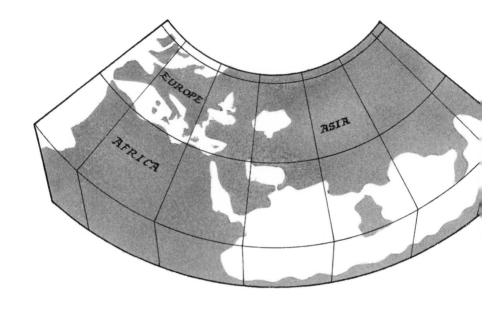

Ptolemy's Map of the Known World

Ptolemy's methods brought new life to mapmaking. His calculations, however, were not correct; his world was about three-fourths of the actual size. But Ptolemy's book was considered one of the best sources of information at that time, and it greatly influenced many thinkers, including Christopher Columbus.

Columbus also exchanged letters with another man who was considering the possibilities of reaching the East by a westward route, Paolo Toscanelli. Toscanelli was a physician, a mathematician, and an astronomer. He sent Columbus a world map he had made. Toscanelli's view of the earth was based on Marco Polo, Ptolemy, and other writers Columbus had read, so his map

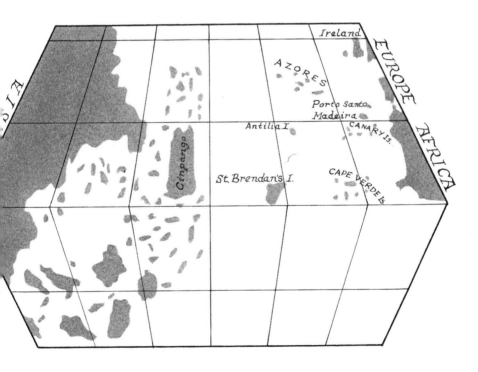

Toscanelli's Map

confirmed what Columbus already believed about the size of the earth and the distance between Europe and Japan.

The Size of the Earth

By the time of Columbus, most educated people had come to understand that the earth was round. How did they know this? People have always tried to make sense of the world. They observed the rising and setting of the sun and the phases of the moon. They noticed that they never seemed to get any closer to the sun, no matter how far east or west they traveled. They saw that the moon and stars seem to cross the sky from east to west. And the stars traveled in patterns. One star, the North Star, didn't move. It stayed in the same place in the northern sky. The stars near it seemed to move in a circle around it. But as people traveled north or south, new stars appeared over the horizon ahead and others disappeared below the horizon behind. If the earth was flat, they reasoned, we would see the same stars from anyplace on earth.

People observed that when ships sailed out from port, in whatever direction they traveled, the hull, or main body of the ship, vanished before the sails did. If the earth was flat, the whole ship would appear smaller and smaller, become a dot, and disappear.

Lunar eclipses were carefully studied. During an

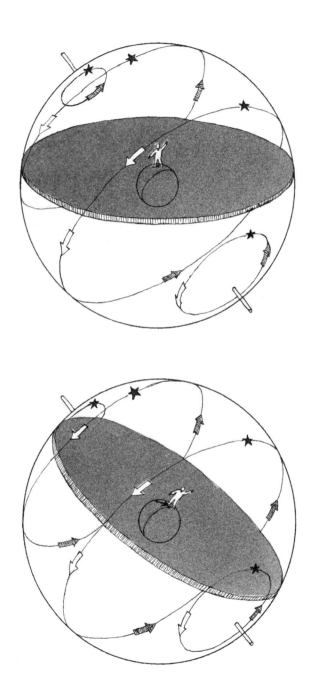

eclipse, the earth casts a shadow on the moon. No matter where the moon was during the eclipse, the earth's shadow, as it moved across the moon, was always curved like part of a circle. To educated people, the only explanation that fit all the things they had observed was that the earth must be a sphere.

People also realized that wherever they were on that sphere, they were never in danger of falling off. People and all the things around them are attracted to the center of the earth. These ideas had been accepted by

Observations of Three Different Lunar Eclipses

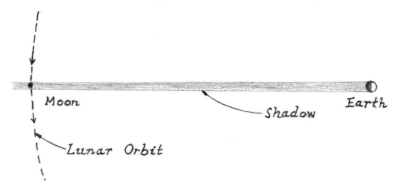

Moon

Shadow

Earth

Lunar Orbit

scholars since the time of the Greeks. What thinking people did not agree on was the size of that sphere. As early as the third century B.C., a Greek mathematician and geographer, Eratosthenes, had calculated the earth's circumference with amazing accuracy. His unit of measurement was a stade. Although we do not know exactly what a stade meant at that time, all likely guesses of its value bring his calculation very close to what is now the accepted figure, 40,076 kilometers. Ptolemy, in his book, used a figure of about 29,000 kilometers for the circumference of the earth. His calculation was accepted by scholars for more than a thousand years.

Columbus tried to verify the size of the earth by making his own computation. If the value of one degree could be determined, that could be multiplied by 360, the number of degrees in a circle, to calculate the circumference of the earth at the equator. The method used for measuring a degree at that time was to figure out the latitude of two points on the same meridian. A meridian is an imaginary line from pole to pole. Places on the same meridian are due north or south of each other. Then the actual distance between the two points was measured and divided by the number of degrees of latitude between them. This gave the length of one degree.

Columbus was able to measure places at greater distances than had been possible in earlier calculations. With the explorations of the west coast of Africa, it became possible for the first time in history to make measurements on a much larger scale. If the same values were arrived at with new measurements, the results should be more convincing. Unfortunately the methods for measuring latitudes and distances were still very inaccurate. And there was often confusion about the standard of measurement being used. Columbus's measurements, which were not accurate, confirmed again his belief that eastern Asia was only a moderate distance west of Europe.

The Distance Across the Atlantic

If the earth was as large as Eratosthenes had said, there were no ships at that time that could carry enough supplies and sail fast enough to travel across the ocean. Columbus accepted a smaller figure for the earth's size. He said that the earth was about 30,000 kilometers, or 20,400 nautical miles, at the equator. The nautical mile is the measure used by navigators. Its length is 6,080 feet, compared to 5,280 feet for an ordinary statute mile. Columbus also believed that the land distance from Europe to the easternmost coast of Asia was greater than it is. He thought that only about one-seventh of the earth was water. And from this he concluded that the ocean was approximately 4,500 kilometers, or 3,000 nautical miles, at the equator. Then he calculated the distance he would have to travel from the Canary Islands to Japan as about 2,400 nautical

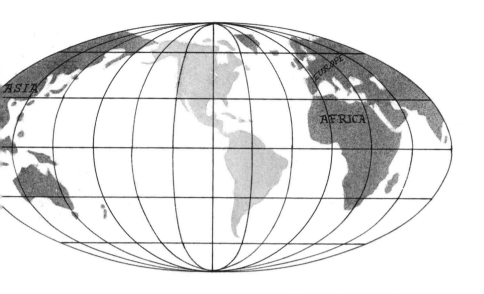

The World as It Really Is

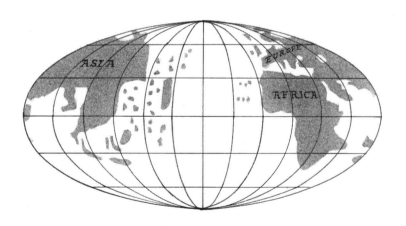

Columbus's Conception of the Earth

miles (Toscanelli's estimate was about 3,000). The distance is actually about 10,600 nautical miles.

Winds and Currents

The scholarly information Columbus was able to gather was more a collection of opinions and disagreements than known facts. But when it came to studying the sea, his genius as a navigator took over. The oceans have more or less permanent currents that are set in motion by prevailing winds, by differences in temperature, and by variations in the salt content of seawater. The use of currents and winds would be of enormous importance in crossing the Atlantic with sails.

Columbus studied the ocean currents and the prevailing winds. These could best be observed from the Azores, Madeira, and the Canaries. Columbus was probably acquainted with the Atlantic for about one thousand miles west of Madeira from his own journeys and from reports of other sailors. He knew he needed to make the greatest possible distance westward in the least possible time or the crew would become frightened. For the outward voyage there was a belt of calms to be avoided and a system of favorable winds to help. Columbus did not sail due west when he left Spain, but went southwest and stopped at the Canary Islands. From there, he could take advantage of the northeast trade winds and avoid the belt of calms between the

Azores and the Canaries. The stopover was necessary because some repairs were needed on the ships, but it also made the ocean voyage shorter. By taking a northern route on the way back, Columbus again took advantage of favorable winds and currents.

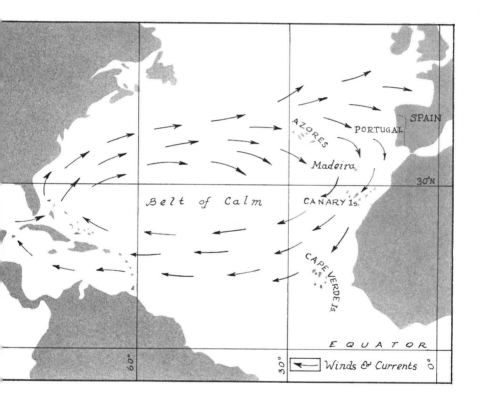

Secret Evidence

Some people believe that Columbus had some secret information. There have been stories of an unknown pilot who, before he died, told Columbus of his ship's being driven by a storm to an island westward in the Ocean Sea. Some people think Columbus had a map of new lands that he carefully guarded. Some even think he had already discovered some lands by sailing west and was now trying to get titles, honors, and riches from a European monarch. It is hard to believe that he gave up everything for eight years just to pursue his Great Enterprise. It is hard to believe that he was able to navigate this voyage so well unless he held some more information.

But Columbus was a man who had complete dedication to his idea, enormous persistence, and an exceptional sense of the sea. The existence of two vast oceans separated by two large continents, rather than just one Ocean Sea, was still unknown to Europeans in 1492. Columbus died without ever fully grasping the truth.

Columbus was one of the foremost mariners of the age of sails. He used every factor that could help and avoided the obstacles that would have held back his progress. With a reliable ship, a competent crew, adequate supplies, and a means of finding the way, Columbus was absolutely sure he could reach his goal and return again.

The Means

CHAPTER FOUR

Government Support and Financing

The cost of ships, a crew, and supplies meant huge expenses. Anything that involved the discovery of new territories and foreign trade automatically involved governments. Any honors, titles, and rights to profits from these ventures could be granted only by a government. No private investor would risk his money on such an enterprise without being sure that the government supported it. Without the backing of some country, Columbus had no hope of pursuing his Great Enterprise.

In 1484, when Columbus was thirty-three years old, he managed to get an audience with King John II of Portugal, who seemed to be the most promising ruler to approach. Portugal had been interested in exploration since the time of Henry the Navigator. Columbus presented the information he had gathered and proposed an expedition to sail west rather than trying to sail around Africa. King John appointed a royal commission to look into Columbus's theories. The commission did not think the plan was possible. But King John was interested and secretly sent out two of his own ships to investigate the idea. The ships returned after being tossed about by winds, also finding the project impossible.

In 1485 Columbus went to Spain to present his proposal to King Ferdinand and Queen Isabella. Columbus was in debt, his wife had died, and he had a young son to support. Spain was fighting a war with the Moors, Muslims from North Africa who had ruled much of Spain since the eighth century. The King and Queen

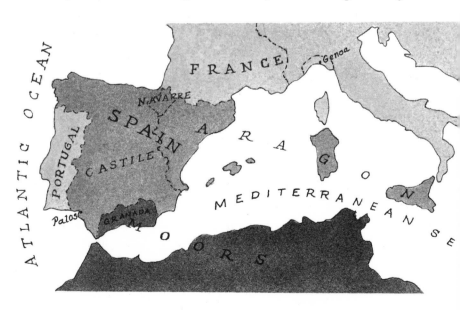

could not do anything to help at that time, but they did listen to Columbus's plan. In return for the vast fortune he was sure he was offering them, Columbus asked for titles, honors, privileges, and a percentage of the profits — all to be passed on to his heirs forever.

The King and Queen also set up a special commission to consider Columbus's proposal. The scholars and seamen who studied the project were all in agreement: Columbus's plan was impossible, and his demands were unreasonable. They argued that the world was much larger than Columbus had calculated, and that no fleet of ships could stay at sea long enough to reach the Indies by sailing west across the ocean. They were, as we know, correct. If there had been no continent between Europe and Asia, Columbus probably would not have been heard of again. But he was also correct that there was land that could be reached by ship; he had seen evidence that convinced him of this. Ferdinand and, especially, Isabella found the possibilities very tempting. They kept Columbus waiting for years while the war and the discussions went on. Eventually the war was won, and they and their advisors finally agreed that the risk involved in allowing Columbus to try to prove his theories was small compared to what could be gained if he succeeded.

The official documents were worked out and signed in April 1492. A contract called the Capitulations set down the terms of the agreement, granting Columbus all the things he had demanded. He was to be made

Admiral of the Ocean Sea. He was to become Viceroy
of all lands he might discover. One-tenth of all gold,
silver, pearls, and profits from these lands could be kept
for himself. He was given the right to judge any cases
that might come up in connection with these goods.
And in future voyages, he could pay one-eighth of the
expenses and keep one-eighth of the profits. He was
also given a passport showing that he had been sent on
this mission by Spain. He had letters of introduction for
the rulers of the lands he found, including one for the

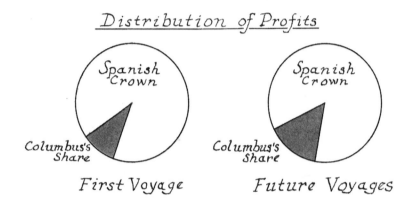

Distribution of Profits

First Voyage   *Future Voyages*

Great Khan of China. There was so little information
about the East at the time that Spaniards were unaware
that no Khan had ruled China since 1368. They also
believed that three small vessels and ninety men could
sail to Japan or China and simply take over, claiming it
for Spain.

Spain officially sponsored and financed this enterprise. Stories have been told that the Queen pawned

her jewels to pay for the voyage. Actually she said to one of her advisors that she was willing to offer her jewels to get a loan, but was assured that this was not necessary. The crown borrowed money from private investors and bankers. The town of Palos had committed an offense and had been fined the use of two ships. Orders were sent for the town to provide Columbus with the two ships as payment of this fine. The third ship and the rest of his provisions were to be supplied at reasonable prices. Anyone charged with a crime would have his trial or punishment suspended if he agreed to sail with Columbus. Now Columbus had to deal with the practical matters of equipping a voyage of exploration.

Reliable Ships

For exploration Columbus needed sturdy, stable ships that could withstand being tossed about by the strong winds and huge waves of the deep oceans. But the ships also had to be able to navigate in coastal waters and rivers of the new lands they reached. If a ship was deep-drafted, if too much of the hull was below the waterline, it would be difficult to handle and there would be greater danger of running aground in shallow waters. The ships needed to be large enough to carry supplies for a long voyage, but if the ships were too large, they would require larger crews. And the bigger the crew,

the more food and water needed. This, in turn, would require more storage space. Columbus had no way of knowing if there would be places to stop and take on more stores along the way. Under the uncertain conditions of exploration, it was a good idea to have a ship that could be handled by a small, weakened crew if the food and water ran out before they returned. Sailing ships run on a free power source — the wind. But since the direction and strength of the wind cannot be controlled, it is important to have ships that can sail well under various wind conditions.

Columbus could not have ships specially designed to meet these needs. Two of his ships, the *Niña* and the *Pinta*, were furnished by the town of Palos to comply with the orders of the King and Queen. Columbus had to find a third, with an owner willing to risk his ship for such an undertaking. The one he chartered, the *Santa María*, became his flagship because she was somewhat larger than the others. Spanish ships at that time had two names. The official name was usually religious, and there was also a nickname — a feminine form of her owner's name, the port she came from, or some sailing quality. The *Niña* was officially named *Santa Clara,* but was called *Niña* after her owner, Juan Niño. Because *niña* means "little girl" in Spanish, she is generally believed to have been the smallest of the fleet. She was probably about the same size as, or only slightly smaller than, the *Pinta.* The official names of the *Pinta* and *Santa María* are not known. The *Santa María* was built in Galicia and nicknamed *La Gallega.* After selecting her as his flagship, Columbus renamed her *Santa María.*

Shipbuilding techniques at that time were passed on from father to son. Construction plans were not drawn. Captains and pilots often gave their opinions about how a ship handled. But new ships were developed by trial and error, and changes came very slowly.

Columbus knew that the three-masted ships being built could make the journey. They were good deep-

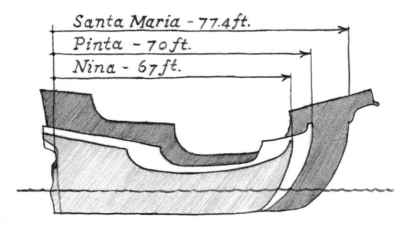

Santa María - 77.4 ft.
Pinta - 70 ft.
Nina - 67 ft.

sea, all-weather ships. The hull, the masts, the rigging, and the sails of a ship worked together as a machine. Each part depended on and helped the others. Weakness in one part could cause damage to another part.

The hull of the ship was made of wood. Oak was often used, since it was a strong hardwood. The shipbuilder started with a framework. First he set the keel, the backbone on which the rest of the frame was built up. Then he bolted the end posts and ribs to the keel to form the skeleton of the ship. When this was complete, he nailed the planks to the frame. Planks were nailed edge to edge, forming a smooth outer surface. The hull was made wide enough to carry a sufficient quantity of food and supplies. The stern, or back end of the ship,

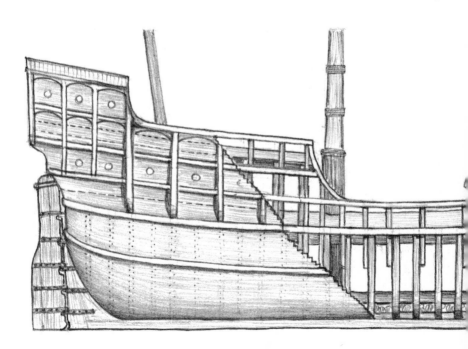

was built higher than the bow, to take rough waves from behind. The ship Columbus sailed, the *Santa María*, probably had a high forecastle, a platform at the front of the ship, which cut down the amount of water thrown over the deck as it sailed into the waves.

Wood swells in water and holds tightly together. Sailors never minded a little water slopping around inside the hull; it kept the ship watertight and safe. The crew washed down the upper decks with salt water at least once a day to keep the wooden planks from shrinking and cracking. There were disadvantages to wooden ships; they rotted easily and made excellent homes for sea worms. To prevent this, the underwater parts of the hull were coated with tar and an animal fat called tallow.

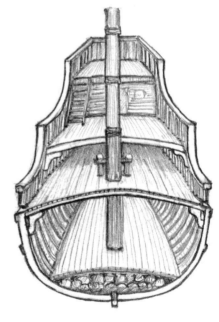

The masts were the tall poles that supported the sails. They were usually made of pine, since pine trees grew tall and straight. The three masts were called the fore, main, and mizzen. On Columbus's ship, the mainmast was taller than the ship was long. The fore- and mizzen-masts were shorter. The masts had to be solid, permanent parts of the boat that did not move. The place where the mast passed through the main deck was the weakest part. It could easily work loose from the pressure of the wind. Mast wedges were used to keep this joint tight. Mast wedges were tapered pieces of wood about 6½ feet (2 meters) long and 2¼ inches (6 centimeters) wide. They were placed upright in a circle around the mast where it entered the deck and were tied tightly.

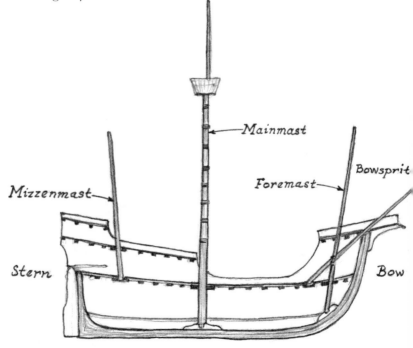

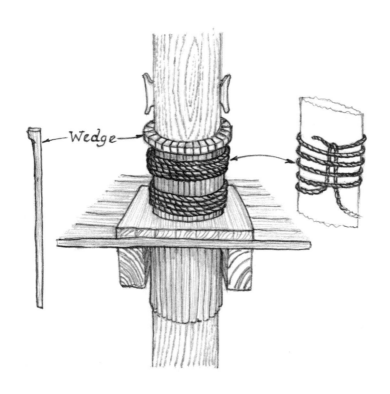

The masts also needed support higher up. The standing rigging was a system of ropes that held the masts steady. The ropes were tarred to keep them firmly in place, but sailors could make some adjustments. The masts had ropes called stays leading forward. The stay from the mainmast ended at the deck and was secured by a deadeye and lanyard. A deadeye was a solid, oval-shaped block of hardwood, often elm. Three holes were bored in it. The end of the stay was attached to one deadeye and another deadeye was fastened to the deck. The lanyard was the short rope joining two deadeyes.

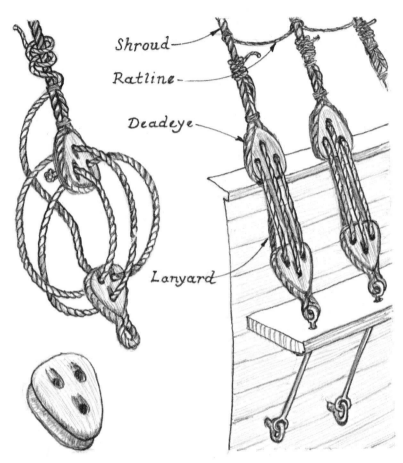

Shroud —
Ratline -
Deadeye -
Lanyard

The stay from the foremast was secured to the bowsprit and helped steady it. The bowsprit was a thin, small mast that was fixed at an angle at the front of the ship. It was attached to a heavy timber on deck and tied to the foremast.

Strong ropes called shrouds secured the masts from side to side. On the fore- and mainmasts, the shrouds were attached to the side of the ship by deadeyes and

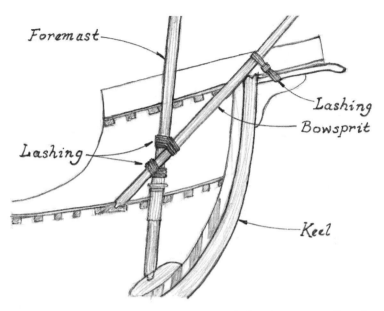

Foremast

Lashing

Lashing

Lashing
Bowsprit

Keel

lanyards. For shrouds, the second deadeye was fixed to a ledge on the outside of the ship. The deadeyes could be drawn together to tighten the shrouds, but it was a job for experts. If the tension was not equal on all parts of the mast, the pole might break. The shrouds on the mizzenmast at the back of the ship were tightened by pulleys fastened on deck. Sometimes smaller ropes were tied across each set of shrouds about fifteen inches apart. They were called ratlines and served as a rope ladder for seamen to climb. The *Santa María* probably had a crow's nest at the top of the mainmast, used for a lookout.

The movable ropes that changed the position of the sails and the yards were called the running rigging. Yards were the long poles across the top of the masts

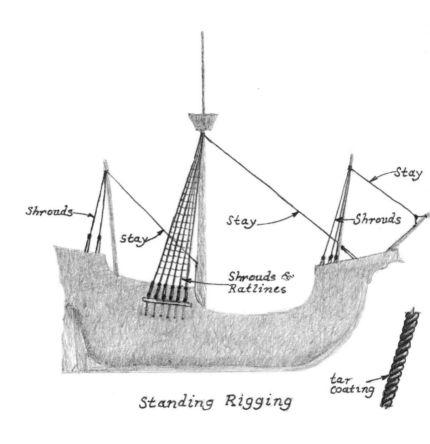

Standing Rigging

from which the sails were hung. It was easy to spot the difference between standing rigging and running rigging. Standing rigging was black from its tar coating and was stretched tightly. Running rigging was not tarred; it was its own natural yellow color and the ropes curved gently. They ran through block and tackles, a system of pulleys that enabled seamen to adjust the sails by tightening or loosening the rigging. Blocks were grooved wooden wheels through which the tackle, the rope, was run. From the blocks, the running rigging was fastened to belaying pins on the deck by twisting

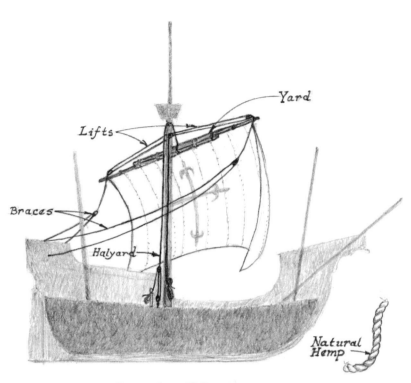

Running Rigging

figure eights about the pin. The running rig could be released at a moment's notice. All rope was made of twisted plant fibers called hemp. Hemp could carry great weight. It did not lose its strength when tarred, and seawater did not make it swell.

The running rigging looked like a complicated web of rope, but each rope was important in controlling the sails. Sailors knew the name and exact position of every rope. Knowing the ropes was a matter of life and death for seamen; their safety depended on being able to find the right rope fast, even in the dark.

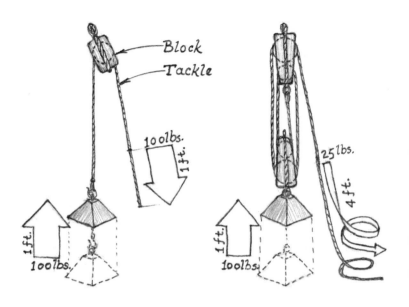

Each sail had ropes that could adjust its position, shape, and size. Hoists or halyards raised and lowered the yards. The parrel, a ring of wooden balls and dividers, held the yard against the mast and helped the yard to move smoothly as it was raised and lowered. Lifts helped keep the yard steady and from swinging up and down. They were also used to help raise the

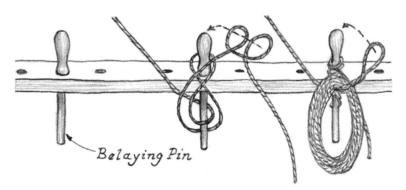

Belaying Pin

yard and support its weight. Braces were used to rotate the yard around the mast. Sheets and tack lines adjusted the lower corners of the sails, keeping them in line with the upper part of the sail or pulling the edges forward if needed. Clew lines raised the lower corners of the sails up to the yard. They were used for rolling up the

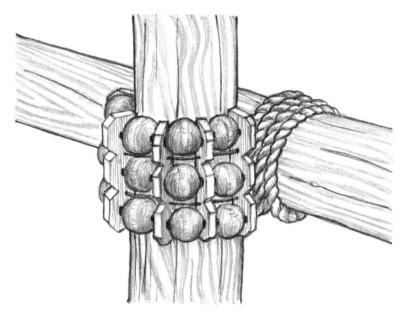

sails and securing them to the yard. This was called furling the sails. They could also be used to raise part of the sail to collect rainwater.

The mizzenmast had a triangular sail called a lateen sail. The rigging was arranged differently, but the ropes did similar jobs to those on a square sail. Ships with lateen sails could sail close into an unfavorable head wind. But a square sail took full advantage of a favor-

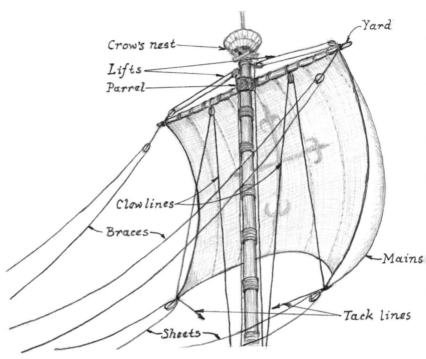

Crow's nest
Lifts
Parrel
Clew lines
Braces
Sheets
Yard
Mains
Tack lines

able wind from behind, at the stern. A lateen sail makes steering more difficult in stern winds because the wind pressure is not evenly distributed across the sail. It is also very difficult work to rotate the yards with a lateen-rigged ship. Of Columbus's fleet, the *Santa María* and the *Pinta* combined both square and lateen sails. The *Niña* was lateen-rigged, but Columbus had the rigging altered when the ships stopped at the Canary Islands.

The sails caught the wind and passed on its power to the hull. The main power came from the largest sail, the mainsail. Wind on the foresail added more power, but it also pushed the front of the ship away from the wind. The lateen sail at the back of the ship could be adjusted to balance these forces.

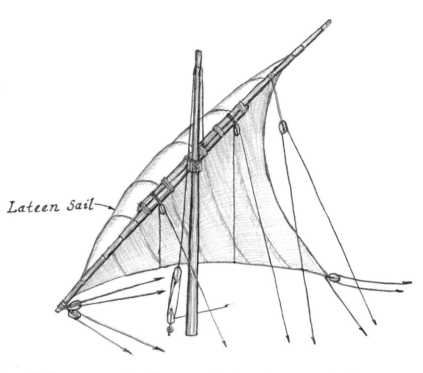

Lateen Sail

Sails were made of canvas. Strips of canvas the length of the sail were overlapped and sewn together. Ships of that time usually had sails decorated with religious symbols. The most popular decoration on Spanish ships was red crosses painted on the white sails. A rope was sewn around the edges of the finished sail to strengthen it. At the lower corners the rope was made into loops to hold the sheets and tack lines.

To sail fast in a favorable wind, the sail area was increased as much as possible. Extra sails could be added too. In addition to the three masts and their sails, the *Santa María* had a light sail on the bowsprit, called the spritsail. It added more pulling power, but could still be balanced by the lateen at the stern. There was a topmast

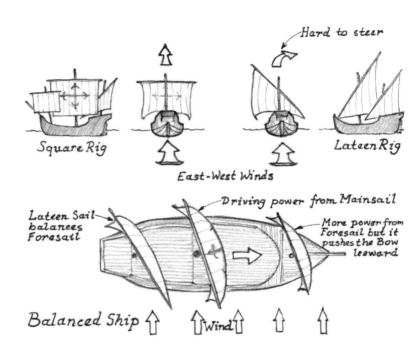

Square Rig

Hard to steer

East-West Winds

LateenRig

Lateen Sail balances Foresail

Driving power from Mainsail

More power from Foresail but it pushes the Bow leeward

Balanced Ship

Wind

above the mainmast. This was more like a flagpole and carried a small square topsail. In Columbus's time the topmast was probably unsupported by stays or shrouds.

Besides adding more sails, the crew could attach extra pieces of sail, called bonnets, to the bottom of the mainsail. The mainsail had rope rings sewn in along the bottom. These were called grommets. The bonnets had loops stitched along the top. Sailors threaded the loops through the grommets when the bonnets were attached. To be sure that the bonnets were put on correctly, the letters *A*, *M*, *G*, and *P* were repeated across the edges of the sail and bonnet. The sailors laced the loops through the grommets with the matching letters while reciting

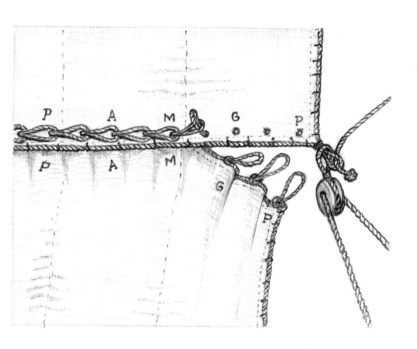

what the letters stood for: Ave Maria Gratia Plena. This meant: Hail Mary, full of grace. This method ensured proper lacing, but it was also a prayer of thanks for the fair winds. Sailing was dangerous, and sailors depended on faith and luck to help them. They used chants and customs in their daily routine to show their faith in God or to bring them good luck.

In fair winds, more sail area would increase the speed of the ship; less sail area would slow the ship down. We know from the log Columbus kept of his first voyage that when he wished to make time, he set all the sails: mainsail with two bonnets, foresail, mizzen, spritsail, and topsail. He even hoisted a sail on the small boats

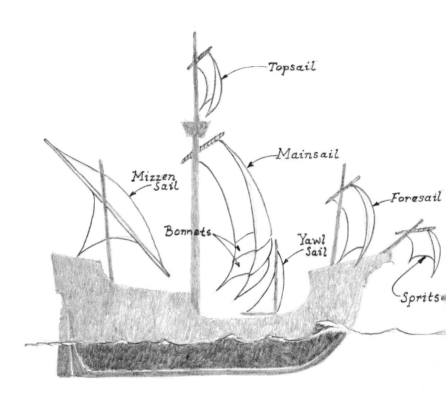

Topsail

Mainsail

Mizzen Sail

Foresail

Bonnets

Yawl Sail

Sprits

stacked on deck. The *Niña* and the *Pinta* sometimes had to shorten their sails so the slower-moving *Santa María* could keep up with them.

It was always important to adjust the sails to the force of the wind, which could be very powerful. When the force was too great for the strength of the equipment, the sails could tear or the masts break. Sometimes the strain on the ship could be so great that the planking of the hull would be stressed to the point that seams burst.

Furling, or rolling up the sails, was a dangerous job requiring many hands. The safest way was to lower the yard as far as possible with the halyard and lifts. Then the wind was spilled from the sail. To do this, about a dozen men hauled the braces to pivot the yard while other men hauled the sheets to move the lower corners of the sail. The yard was turned until it pointed into the wind. When in position, the sail was hoisted to the yard by the clew lines. Sailors bunched up the sail and lashed it to the yard. Then it could be hauled up the mast, out of the way. All this often had to be done while the ship was heaving and huge waves splashed across the deck.

We do not know exactly how Columbus's three ships looked. We have no plans, drawings, or measurements, and little other precise information about them. We do know that Columbus found the *Santa María* clumsy,

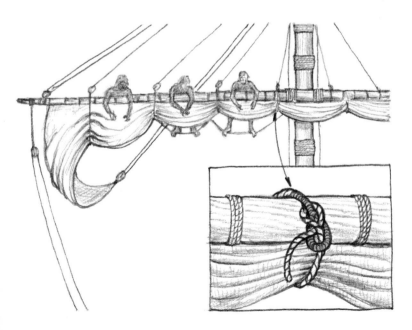

slow, deep-drafted, and difficult to sail. The ship ran aground and sank somewhere off the coast of what is now Haiti on December 24, 1492. The first Christmas in the New World was spent trying to salvage the stores and equipment from the wreckage of the *Santa María*. On the return voyage the *Pinta* and *Niña* had to face fierce storms and the rough seas of the Atlantic in winter. These ships proved to be sturdy and swift. The *Pinta* sailed across the Atlantic several times after that, although not with Columbus. She sank in the year 1500, in a hurricane near Jamaica. The *Niña* was Columbus's favorite. He purchased a share of her, and the *Niña* returned to the New World on Columbus's second voyage. She survived a hurricane and once again brought Columbus safely back to Spain. The *Niña* also carried supplies and passengers on the third voyage.

As the ninety men first sailed across the Atlantic, no one knew they would be making history. The small ships of the fleet creaked and groaned as they rolled and pitched through the ocean. But Columbus and his crew were prepared to face the unknown in these well-built, well-rigged little ships.

A Competent Crew

Columbus needed the help of many people to make his journey. Finding good sailors was as important as finding reliable ships. Columbus chartered the *Santa María* from Juan de la Cosa, a man he knew. De la Cosa agreed to sail as master. As owner of the ship, he probably brought some sailors with him.

Palos had to supply two other ships. The royal order was read in the town on May 23, 1492. Columbus now had three ships and part of a crew, but the sailors of Palos did not want to sign up for the voyage. No one there knew Columbus, and they thought his idea was too dangerous. Local seamen were not convinced that he could sail far enough west to find lands and be able to get back again. They thought he was a dreamer, they knew nothing of his sailing abilities, and they refused to sail with him.

Fortunately Columbus had a friend who was a friar from a nearby monastery. The friar introduced Columbus to one of the best sea captains of Palos, Martín Alonso Pinzón. It was an important meeting. Pinzón could tell that Columbus was an exceptional seaman. He understood the information Columbus had gathered, and believed in his enterprise. He agreed to sail as captain of the *Pinta*, with his brother as captain of the *Niña*. Several of their relatives also signed on. With these well-respected seamen going and with promises of finding gold and riches, many sailors overcame their fear of the Sea of Darkness and joined the crew.

Since the wages of the crew were paid by the Spanish government, payroll records have been traced, and we know the names and jobs of most of the men who sailed with Columbus. Of the ninety men who sailed the three ships, eighty-seven have been identified. Because the King and Queen had offered pardons for criminals who signed up, there are many stories that Columbus sailed with a crew of desperate characters and cutthroats. One man in Palos was to be executed for killing a man in an argument. Three friends tried to help him escape from jail and were also sentenced to death. All four took advantage of the royal offer and enlisted with Columbus. They were the only men convicted of crimes who signed on. The four were pardoned, and two of them sailed on later voyages with Columbus. All in all, it was a hard-working group of seamen who did their jobs well.

The officers on Columbus's ships were the captain, the master, and the pilot. The captain was responsible for everything and everybody. Columbus was captain of the *Santa María* as well as captain of the fleet. He could not officially use the title of admiral until he had successfully completed his mission.

The master was in charge of running the ship and was an advisor to the captain of the fleet. He had to be an excellent seaman. He was in charge of all the sailors. He saw to it that the necessary food and supplies were on board and properly stored. He managed the ship under sail. Often the owner of the ship sailed as master. This was true on the *Santa María* and the *Niña*. On the *Pinta*, another Pinzón brother served as master, and the owner sailed as one of the skilled seamen.

Each ship had a pilot, who was in charge of the navi-

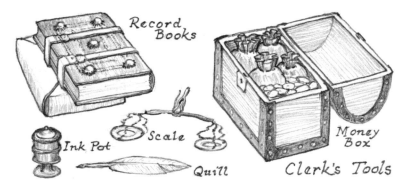

Record Books

Ink Pot Scale

Quill

Money Box

Clerk's Tools

gation. He needed to know about tides and weather. He had to bring his own charts, compass, and instruments. He marked on the chart the estimated position of the ship each day.

Some of the crew were not sailors, but Columbus's fleet had very few that the sailors would have called idlers. Luis de Torres went as an interpreter. He was a Jew who had converted to Catholicism because of the persecution of Jews in Spain. He spoke Hebrew and a little Arabic. Everyone assumed this knowledge would help in communicating with the Japanese and with the Great Khan.

The secretary of the fleet did the paperwork. He prepared reports and wrote official documents of possession for lands discovered. He had nothing to do with keeping the log of the ship; Columbus wrote that himself.

The paymaster, a royal official, kept accounts of expenses and any treasure that was discovered. He kept records of everything that was loaded or unloaded. His job was to look out for royal interests and to be sure

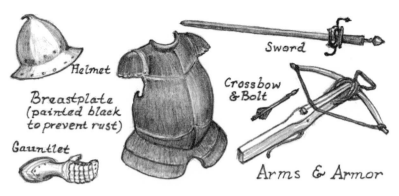

Helmet

Breastplate
(painted black
to prevent rust)

Gauntlet

Sword

Crossbow
& Bolt

Arms & Armor

that the King and Queen got their share of gold, precious stones, and all valuable goods brought back.

Columbus also had a personal steward to serve him. One gentleman volunteer came along, probably just out of curiosity. He may have had hopes of meeting the Great Khan.

The master-at-arms was responsible for discipline on the ship. He punished anyone who didn't obey the rules.

There was a surgeon on each ship. This was someone who knew something about herbs and medicine. He saw to the health of the men on board and brought his own instruments and remedies. There was little need for medical attention on this healthy fleet, but he also served as barber.

The petty officers had special duties. The boatswain carried out the orders of the master and pilot. He supervised the work of the crew, made sure all the supplies were stored properly, inspected the rigging, and saw to it that the cooking fire was out at sunset. He had an experienced seaman to help him, the boatswain's mate.

The steward was another important officer. He was in charge of drinking water, food, wine, candles, and fuel for the firebox. He also kept the key to the storeroom. He had to be sure that older food was used first, that men were awake when on duty, and that prayers were said at the appropriate times.

Able seamen had to do several different jobs on the ship, but many also were specialists at a particular job. On wooden ships it was important to have carpenters to make repairs. Carpenters brought their own tools.

The caulker also brought his tools and his own supply of tar, tallow, oil, and anything else needed to stop a leak. He was in charge of keeping the ship watertight.

The cooper repaired all the casks and barrels, which were used to store food and supplies. It was his job to see that they were kept tight and well stowed or lashed so they would not roll. Coopers did their best to keep the food as dry as possible and to keep out rats, cockroaches, and other small animals that always managed to live on ships.

The pumps needed regular attention. Seawater constantly seeped into even the most watertight ship, and

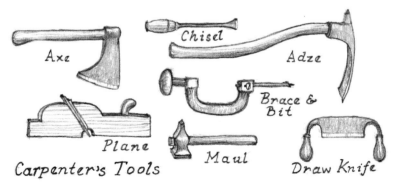

Carpenter's Tools

two pumps were used to get it out. A wooden pipe made of sections of bored-out logs went down to the hold. A leather valve was attached to wooden pump rods. As the valve rose, it pushed up a column of water that spilled out at the top. The valve also became tighter, creating a vacuum that sucked up more water. Whenever the pumps brought up large quantities of clear seawater, it was a sign that the ship had developed a serious leak.

The helmsman steered the ship. He managed the long tiller, which was attached to the rudder on the back of the ship. He had to work in a low, cavelike area under the quarterdeck, and the base of the mizzenmast blocked his view. Orders were shouted down to him from the deck above. He had to know the feel of the tiller and the feel of the ship beneath his feet to judge how to steer.

Columbus's crew also listed a tailor, a painter, and a silversmith. The silversmith would be able to tell the quality and value of all the precious metals they hoped to find. Most seamen worked at jobs as they were

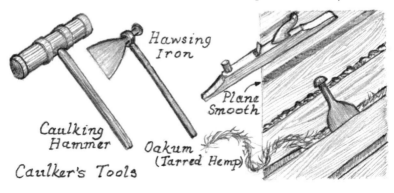

Hawsing
Iron

Plane
Smooth

Caulking
Hammer

Oakum
(Tarred Hemp)

Caulker's Tools

needed. All mariners probably had to know how to repair sails.

Sailors did not wear a special uniform, and they were not provided with clothing. They wore whatever they had. Most wore a loose shirt with a hood and a red wool cap. Another common garment was an overcoat of brown cloth, the warmest piece of clothing a sailor had. Red was a traditional color among seafarers. Columbus

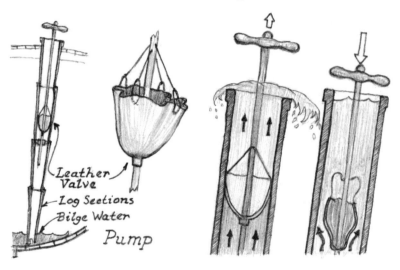

Leather Valve

Log Sections

Bilge Water

Pump

may have often dressed in red. In his log he mentioned giving his red cloak to an Indian chief and also giving him red shoes. Most of the ordinary sailors didn't wear any shoes.

Everyone on the crew had to work hard. They were paid a fixed wage at the usual rate for long voyages. Masters and pilots received 2,000 maravedís a month; able seamen, 1,000; ordinary seamen and ship's boys,

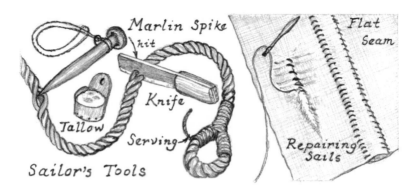

Sailor's Tools

Marlin Spike · hit · Tallow · Knife · Serving

Flat Seam · Repairing Sails

666. The monthly payroll for the three ships totaled 250,180 maravedís. The seamen received four months' pay in advance, and the rest was paid when they returned. If a sailor died on the voyage, his wages would be paid to his heirs. It is difficult to determine a modern value for these wages. At that time, a bushel of wheat cost 73 maravedís; a cow, 2,000 maravedís; a pig, 400; and a duck, 35. The crown allowed 12 maravedís a day for feeding each seaman. Columbus paid the same wages on his fourth voyage, about ten years later.

Adequate Supplies

The ships had enough supplies for at least a year. Columbus expected to be back in much less time than that, and he was trying to be sure there would be enough supplies for the return journey if he failed to find land. The main provisions were water, wine, hard biscuits, bacon, chickpeas, kidney beans, lentils, cheese, and

dried, salted fish and meats. These were the basic foods.
They also brought oil, lard, flour, salt, vinegar, onions,
snap beans, garlic, olives, rice, sugar, honey, almonds,
raisins, figs, and other dried fruits.

It was normal for voyages of exploration to carry
weapons and ammunition. There was always a possibility of fighting with the natives of any land the explorers
found. Columbus's ships probably had some small
weapons — bombards or small cannons, swivel guns

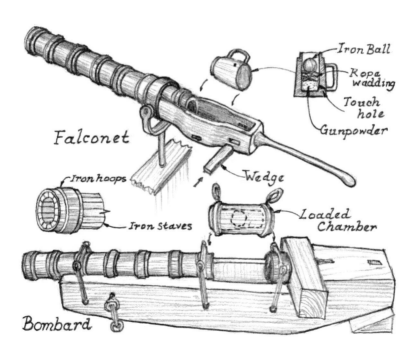

Falconet

Iron Ball

Rope wadding

Touch hole

Gunpowder

Iron hoops

Iron staves

Wedge

Loaded Chamber

Bombard

mounted on the side of the ship called falconets, crossbows, swords, lances, and hand-held muskets called *espingardas*. They also brought some armor — helmets, breastplates, and shields. But Columbus's fleet was not really equipped for conquering or fighting, only for exploration.

Columbus brought merchandise for trade or gifts. This was a supply of trinkets — small mirrors, glass beads, brooches, bells, colored hats — that had appealed to natives other explorers had encountered. All the cargo had to be stowed in the hold below the main deck along with extra sails and rope.

Space was very limited. Many men had to live, eat, work, and sleep on these small ships. Only the captain had a cabin to himself. The *Santa María* had a raised castle at the stern. This was formed by the quarterdeck over the main deck, and the small poop deck above that. Columbus's cabin was at the stern, on the quarterdeck. It was a small room with little furniture: a bed, a washing stand, a table with his own tableware, a desk, a stool, and a chest containing navigational charts and documents. He probably had shields, armor, and his sword displayed, as well as the flags that the ships might fly on formal occasions. The *Santa María* hoisted the flag of Castile and León, the two parts of Spain united by the marriage of Ferdinand and Isabella. It was divided into quarters, with yellow castles on a red background, and red lions with yellow crowns on a white background.

The fleet had a special flag, white with a green cross in the center and crowned initials of the King and Queen. Columbus brought his own navigational equipment — astrolabe, quadrant, and compass. Since he was a devout Catholic, he had a rosary and an image of the Virgin Mary.

The master and the pilot may have had narrow cabins in the hold. These would have been little more than closets. Other officers bunked on storage cupboards under the quarterdeck, out of the way of the tiller. The senior mariners would settle under the shelter of the quarterdeck. The boatswain, surgeon, and master-at-arms would claim space near the open end but still under shelter.

The *Santa María* also had a raised deck, called the forecastle deck, at the bow of the ship above the main deck. The carpenter, caulker, and some other able seamen probably settled under the forecastle. There were long, low lockers for storing their tools which could also be used as bunks.

The rest of the crew could use any space left over. Some might manage to get under shelter, but most would have to sleep on mats on the open deck. When not in use, their sleeping mats had to be rolled away and stowed in the hold. Usually sailors were not permitted to sleep in the hold because they were supposed to be at hand for any emergency. This may not have been required on the *Santa María* because there was such a large crew. The sailors had to find a place that could be their home for months to come, yet not be in the way of the routine working of the ship.

The main deck was crowded, with the tiller, the masts, the compass box, hatches for getting down into the hold, spare anchors, sails and yards, barrels, the windlass for hauling up the anchor, the pumps, weapons, and sweeps — the long oars that were sometimes needed. Each sweep was manned by as many as four sailors, who rowed by walking back and forth. There were also two small boats with their own oars and sails stowed on the main deck. The larger one was called the launch. It took up most of the length of the deck between the forecastle and the quarterdeck, and was used for heavy work — loading and unloading supplies or laying out anchors. It took about fifty full loads of the launch to fill the hold. The smaller boat, called the yawl, was placed on top of it. It was used for going from ship to ship or for rowing to land.

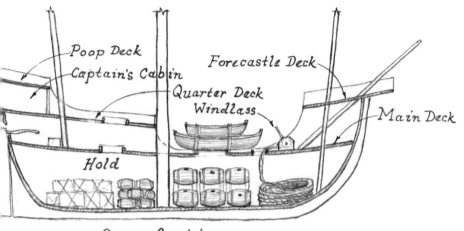

Poop Deck
Captain's Cabin
Forecastle Deck
Quarter Deck
Windlass
Main Deck
Hold

Cross Section

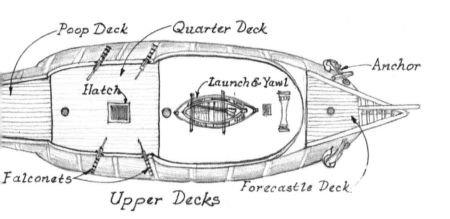

Poop Deck
Quarter Deck
Anchor
Hatch
Launch & Yawl
Falconets
Forecastle Deck

Upper Decks

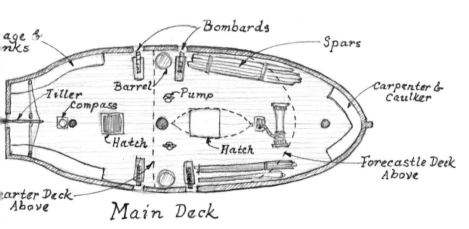

age &
nks
Bombards
Spars
Barrel
Carpenter &
Caulker
Tiller
Compass
Pump
Hatch
Hatch
Forecastle Deck
Above
arter Deck
Above

Main Deck

With all that was crowded onto the ship, there had to be a limit to the amount of personal belongings a crew member could bring. Extra clothing and other items were carried in chests. The size of the chest was set in relation to rank. Captains and pilots were allowed a chest not bigger than five palms in length by three in height. (A palm was a measure of length from the thumb to the end of the little finger with fingers extended.) Two sailors had to share one chest between them, three apprentices shared one, and the ship's boys made do with one among four of them.

Instruments to Find the Way

COMPASS

The most important instrument to Columbus and his pilots was the magnetic compass. On the open sea when clouds blocked out the sun and stars, the compass was the only thing that showed the direction they were going. It was the most reliable instrument on board and the one they could not navigate without.

The compass consisted of a round card on which was marked the compass rose of thirty-two points. The card was mounted on a brass pivot in a wooden bowl so that it could rotate freely. A magnetized needle or wire was attached underneath the card between the north and south marks. The needle was magnetized by stroking it with a lodestone, a naturally magnetic ore. Retouching the wire was necessary to keep it magnetized. Plenty of spare needles were brought, and the pilot guarded the lodestone with his life.

A black line called the lubber line was drawn on the edge of the bowl. The needle always pointed north, so the point on the card at the lubber line showed the direction the ship was headed. The lubber line had to line up with the keel of the ship, its central line, to show the ship's direction accurately. The compass was kept in a rectangular box called a binnacle, to hold it in a fixed position on the rolling ship. The binnacle was fastened to the deck or to a solid table lashed to the deck. It was illuminated at night by a lantern hanging from the beam above. The table was on the main deck in front of the tiller for the helmsman to steer by.

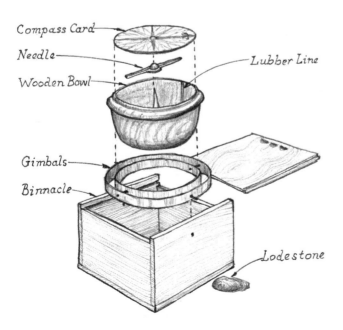

Compass Card
Needle
Wooden Bowl
Lubber Line
Gimbals
Binnacle
Lodestone

Modern compasses have letters for the directions and degree markings. On Columbus's ships the sailors read the compass by the length, shape, and color of the points on the compass rose: north was marked by a fleur-de-lis; east was sometimes shown by a cross, since the Holy Land is in the East.

The magnetic compass is not as simple to use or as accurate as it would seem. Errors in the mounting of the compass, like an off-center pivot, might go unnoticed. The magnetic poles of the earth are not at the same place as the geographic poles. The difference is called the magnetic variation, and the significance of this difference depends on the location on earth. The existence of magnetic variation was known, although not completely understood. Columbus observed the variation and noted it in his log on September 13. Some

of the men were afraid that their only reliable instrument was becoming unreliable, but Columbus remained calm and kept the crew calm. Compass north could be compared with the North Star to correct their direction. The pilot raised his right hand to sight the star, then brought it down on the rim of the compass box. This was known as the pilot's blessing.

SAND GLASS

Measuring time was important in running the ship, to regulate work shifts and calculate the distance made good at the speed traveled. On Columbus's ships, time was measured by sand glasses. The sand glass was made of two glass bulbs, one above the other. A small piece of metal pierced with a tiny hole was placed between them. The joint was sealed with wax and wrapped with canvas and thread. Then the glass was set in a wooden stand. It took a half hour for all the sand inside to fall from the top to the bottom bulb. The instrument was fragile, so many spares were carried on a ship.

Men worked in four-hour watches. There would be eight half-hour glasses to each watch. The ship's boy on duty called out when the last of the sand fell into the bottom of the glass and quickly turned it over. He was a talking clock for the ship. He announced the time by calling, "One glass is gone and now the second floweth," or, "Six glasses have gone and now the seventh floweth."

It was not a very accurate way of keeping time. As the ship rolled with the sea, the flow of sand would be uneven. In hot weather, the glass would expand and sand would flow through the neck slightly faster. Over time the grains would rub against the metal hole, wearing it away and slightly increasing its size. A ship's boy who wanted to shorten his watch could turn the glass before all the sand was out or warm the glass between his hands to make the sand flow faster, but he risked severe punishment.

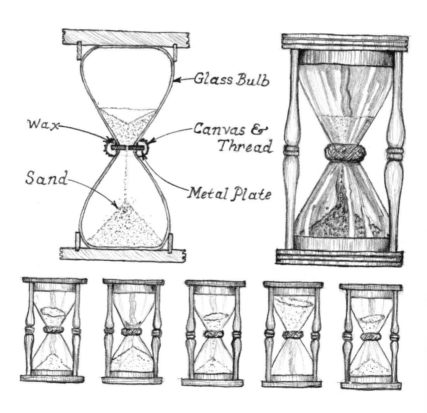

The sand glass could be corrected to local noontime by noting when the sun was due south. A pin was placed near the center of the compass card and the glass was turned as soon as the shadow touched the fleur-de-lis.

Columbus also used the stars to tell time. The two brightest stars of the Little Dipper appear to move completely around the North Star every twenty-four hours. One of these was known as a Guard. Early navigators imagined a man with the North Star at his middle and eight positions around him. The Guard would move

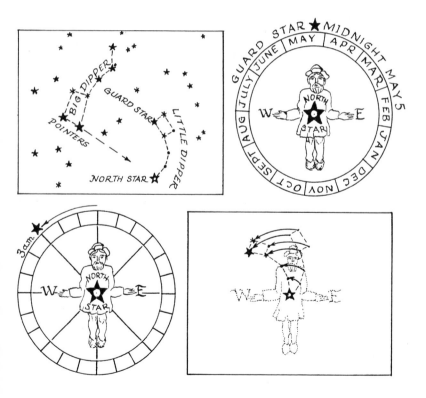

counterclockwise, one position every three hours. By knowing the position of the Guard for midnight on a particular date, it was possible to figure out the time by this celestial clock. If the Guard was at Head at midnight on that day, it would be at West Shoulder at 3 A.M. and time to call the watch. Columbus mentioned using this method of telling time in his log entry of September 30.

SOUNDING LEAD

It was important to know if the ship was nearing land or shallow places where it might run aground. An essential instrument for navigation was the sounding lead. This was a cone-shaped lead weight attached to a knotted line. It was lowered to measure the depth of the water. The knots marked fathoms, a measure of about six feet. A standard length of lead line was forty fathoms, but all the ships in the fleet had a deep-sea lead line of one hundred fathoms.

On September 16 the mariners found themselves sailing in a dense mass of floating seaweed. They were in a part of the ocean known as the Sargasso Sea. At first they had hopes that they were near land, since seaweed is usually found near land. Columbus also had seen songbirds, which he expected to find only near shore. The crew sounded with the lead, then with two lines of rope tied together. The lead did not touch bottom.

They became alarmed. Seaweed covered the ocean as far as they could see. Sailors had heard legends of ships entangled in a net of seaweed with monsters lurking in its depths. It was up to Columbus to remain calm and keep his crew from panicking. He was determined to keep sailing. The water was deep and the weed did not keep them from moving along steadily. Soon they just got used to it. The fleet sailed on. Columbus was not the first seaman to discover the Sargasso Sea, but he was the first to accurately report that there was no danger in crossing it.

A good navigator made frequent use of his sounding lead when he was approaching land or thought land might be near. The lead had a recess at the bottom that was filled with tallow. Some of the mud and sand from

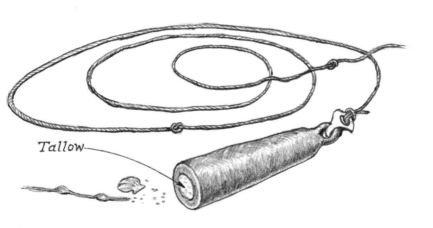

Tallow

the seabed would stick to the tallow. This sample was an important source of information for the pilot. The mud picked up by the sounding lead varied in color, texture, taste, and smell. Many seamen could navigate familiar waters in heavy fog by taste and smell alone. An experienced pilot could tell by a sample of the seabed when the ship was nearing land and when it was in danger. Columbus was usually careful about taking soundings, but in the deep, clear waters of the Bahamas, carelessness led to the loss of the *Santa María*.

QUADRANT

With only limited instruments available, the navigators of the fifteenth century had to use their senses to find their way. They believed what they could see. They understood the earth was round, but saw the earth as the center of all things. They saw the stars as a dome above them that seemed to move around the earth in regular patterns. Knowledge of these patterns could help a navigator. As we have seen, stars could be used as a timekeeper. Orion, an important constellation, could be used as a direction finder. The central stars in Orion's belt are due east and west when rising and setting.

Stars could also be used as position finders. The North Star — also known as Polaris, the Pole Star, and Stella Maris, the Star of the Sea — was the most impor-

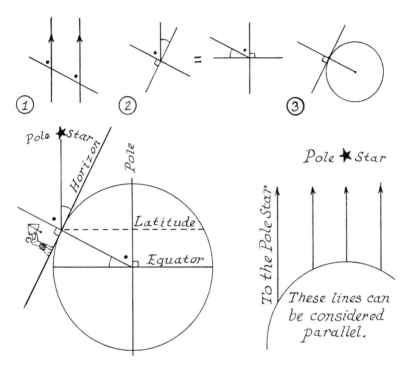

tant star to sailors. Positioned above the North Pole, it is a faint star that can be seen only in the northern hemisphere. The height of the North Star above the horizon gave the approximate latitude of the observer, or how far north of the equator the ship was. If the Pole Star was on the horizon, the ship was on the equator. If it was 29 degrees above the horizon, the ship was at about 29 degrees north latitude, the latitude of the Canary Islands. Using the instruments available on firm land, a navigator could expect to find his latitude with reasonable accuracy. The problem was getting an accurate means of measuring at sea. An error of one degree in the reading meant an error of about sixty miles in latitude. One of the tools used for measurements at sea was the quadrant.

The quadrant was a quarter-circle made of wood. There were two pinholes along one straight edge through which the North Star was sighted and a scale of 90 degrees along the curved side. A small weight attached to a silk thread hung from the point where the two straight sides met. The quadrant was held in the hand, and when the star was sighted through the pinholes, someone would note the degree mark where the thread crossed the arc.

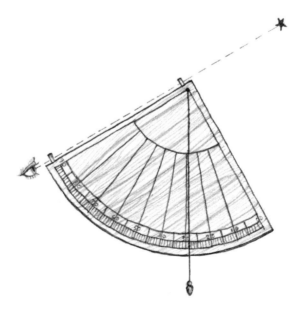

Columbus made some use of a quadrant, but there were many problems with this tool. One was that the North Star does not mark the pole exactly; it makes a small daily revolution around it, and adjustments had to be made. A greater problem was that it was almost impossible to get an accurate reading on a constantly rocking ship.

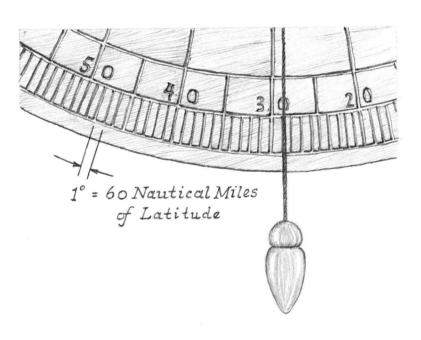

1° = 60 Nautical Miles of Latitude

Columbus also carried another instrument for finding position. The mariner's astrolabe had been developed for conditions at sea. It was made of brass and consisted of a large graduated circle. An alidade, a straight piece with two sighting holes, was attached at its center. A ring at the top was either held by the thumb with the arm outstretched or hung by a rope from the mainmast. The astrolabe was heavy — ten to twelve pounds — so that it could be used in wind, and much of its surface was cut away so there was little to be caught by the wind. When the navigator sighted the North Star, he could

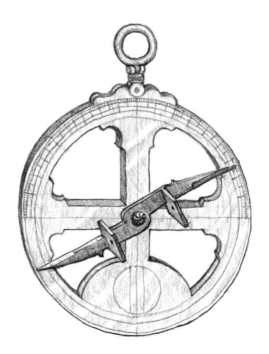

read the altitude by where the alidade crossed the circle, and so determine his latitude.

As ships sailed farther south, the North Star appeared close to the horizon and became difficult to use for fixing a latitude. The astronomers of the Royal Observatory in Spain calculated the height of the sun above the equator at noon for every day of the year, for four years in advance. Using a book of tables, a navigator could also figure out his latitude from the altitude of the sun at noon.

Finding latitude by using the North Star presented many difficulties, but using the sun caused even more. Altitude could only be taken at one time of day, noon, when the sun was at its highest point. The sun could not be sighted directly or the observer would damage his eyes. Since timekeeping was not accurate, the observation had to start before noon and continue until the sun reached its highest point. The observer could only hope that the ship would be steady enough at that moment to get a reading. Sightings were impossible when clouds obscured the sun or the stars.

The astrolabe could also be used for taking the altitude of the sun. For observing the sun, the instrument had to be held until the sun's rays passed through both holes on the sight rule and cast a spot of light on a surface held behind it. This could more easily be done with the astrolabe hanging from its ring than with the quadrant grasped in the hand. But the mariner's astrolabe was a difficult instrument to use on a ship even in

very calm conditions. Most seamen were able to use these instruments with accuracy only when they reached land.

Some historians have written that the invention of the astrolabe enabled Columbus to discover America. But in his log he mentioned early on that he had an astrolabe but was not able to use it. In fact, he had decided it was broken and stowed it for the remainder of the voyage. Mostly he judged by eye the altitude of the North Star against the masts to make a rough estimate of his latitude. He had to rely on other means to determine his position on the chart more accurately.

MAPS AND CHARTS

The seaman's chart that Columbus brought was drawn on a large piece of sheepskin. Charts made of animal hides were sturdier and less likely to fall apart at sea. The coasts of Europe, North Africa, the Azores, Madeira, and the Canary Islands were drawn in as accurately as possible. Even though governments like Spain's and Portugal's were trying to establish standardized charts, early maps differed. Sailors described what they had seen to a mapmaker, and he did his best to interpret this correctly on his map. As we have seen, latitude was difficult to measure accurately, and mariners had no means to figure out longitude at that time — how far east or west they were. Even the position of the equator varied from map to map. Much about the

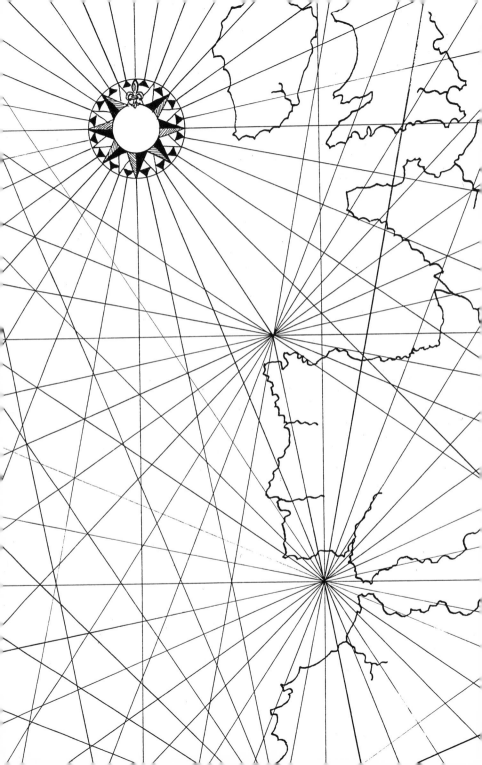

world was still unknown, and conceptions about geography were changing rapidly.

Known areas were mapped as accurately as possible, then uncharted coasts were drawn from estimations. Cipango and Cathay were sketched in where Columbus and many scholars calculated them to be. Columbus's map would have also shown him islands believed to exist in the Atlantic which might serve as steppingstones to the Indies. Legendary places like Saint Brendan's Island and Antilia were drawn on most maps of that time.

Martin Behaim constructed one of the earliest globes in 1492. Although Columbus probably never saw the globe, it is possible that he was familiar with Behaim's work. Martin Behaim was a scholar from Nuremberg, Germany, who lived in Portugal from 1484 to 1487. He was appointed to the royal commission, but was not serving during the time Columbus's plan for the Great Enterprise was being considered. Columbus and Behaim could have met while they were both in Portugal, but there is no positive evidence that their paths ever crossed.

Behaim returned to Germany to construct a globe commissioned by the city of Nuremberg. He built a beautiful one showing a world very close to Columbus's conception. Behaim had the same wrong ideas based on the same sources. Europe and Asia were drawn much closer than they really are, and of course the existence of North and South America was not known. Behaim placed Saint Brendan's Island about halfway across the Atlantic.

In 1493, after Columbus had returned from his expedition believing he had reached the Indies, Behaim returned to Portugal with a letter from a friend of King John II. The letter suggested a plan for sailing west to the Indies, citing the same evidence for the existence of western land within sailing distance as Columbus used in his proposal. It told King John that Martin Behaim was ready to set sail from the Azores and take charge of this voyage. Behaim may also have brought a sketch of his globe.

It is doubtful that this letter was written without knowledge of Columbus's return; the news had certainly reached Nuremberg. It is more likely that it was a political move to claim that King John had earlier plans for a westward voyage and that Columbus had used Behaim's information. Behaim's globe was so similar to Columbus's view of the world that it might suggest they had worked together. But the idea of sailing west to reach the East had been in the air at least eighteen years before Columbus set sail — Toscanelli's map was made in 1474. If Columbus had failed, someone else would have embarked on the same adventure. But Martin Behaim planned to start the voyage from the Azores, where he would have been forced to fight the strong westerly winds.

Columbus knew not to make that mistake, but he was in unknown territory for most of his journey. By the standards of the times, he had an unusually well-equipped and well-organized fleet for exploration and the best technology available. He was sure he knew where he was on his map and exactly where he was going.

The Journey

CHAPTER FIVE

Finding the Way

When Columbus was at sea, crossing unknown ocean waters without landmarks of any kind and only primitive instruments to aid him, he was at his best. At sea the only thing he could really depend on was his own skill as a sailor. He knew the feel of his ships, and he relied on his memory and experience to guide him through any difficulties he might encounter. Many people who knew Columbus commented that he had an exceptionally keen sense of smell. They said he was able to distinguish different kinds of perfume. He also had excellent eyesight and hearing. He kept careful watch of the ship, wind, sea, and sky, and had a reputation for being a very good weather forecaster. Sights, sounds, smells, tastes, depth of water, and the consistency of the ocean bottom were all important in finding the way. Columbus ventured into unknown parts of the sea with such confidence because he understood the sea. As navigational instruments grew more precise, the skills and senses of the sailors using them became less important. But when Columbus sailed, he had to trust his instincts above all.

He navigated by dead reckoning. This was a method of plotting the position of the ship by using the distance sailed and the course steered. From the known starting place, the navigator would take the course steered, the time traveled, the speed traveled, and figure the distance traveled. Taking into consideration the currents and drift of the ship, he would determine the position of the ship after the day of sailing. This would be marked on the map. From this new starting place, he would again calculate his position at the end of the next day. The latitude was taken as often as possible to check the accuracy of these figures. As we have seen, there were instruments to measure direction and latitude with some accuracy. Speed and distance were mostly judged by experience. Seamen relied a great deal on knowing the feel of their ship under varying conditions and wind directions.

To check speed, they dropped a piece of wood overboard at the bow and watched it drift past. Sometimes they paced the deck alongside the floating object. Or they timed how long it took for the object to pass the length of the ship by reciting a chant or rhyme or with

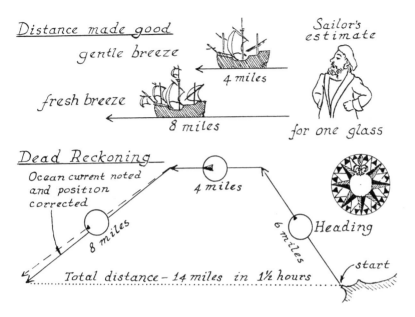

Distance made good
gentle breeze
4 miles
for one glass

Sailor's estimate

fresh breeze
8 miles

Dead Reckoning
Ocean current noted and position corrected
4 miles
8 miles
6 miles
Heading
start
Total distance — 14 miles in 1½ hours

a small sand glass. Of course tides and currents were moving both the object and the ship in any of a number of directions.

The navigator had no instrument to measure distance at sea; he was supposed to know his ship. When sailing in coastal waters, where there were known distances and landmarks, the navigator developed a feel for the speed and distance a ship was making. Fifteenth-century seamen had a remarkable ability to estimate distance by dead reckoning.

A traverse board was used to keep track of the dead reckoning. This was a simple nautical calculator. A round wooden board showed the thirty-two points of the compass. Eight peg holes along each point represented each half hour of the four-hour watch. Pegs were inserted to show the course steered every half hour, marking from the center outward. If the course for the first half hour of the watch was due west, a peg was put into the first hole west of center. If the course changed to west by north during the next half hour, a peg was placed in the second hole on the west-by-north line.

Below the compass rose there were eight horizontal grooves with about ten holes in each. Each hole represented one mile per hour. If the navigator thought the ship had been making four miles per hour in the first half hour, he would put a peg into the fourth hole of

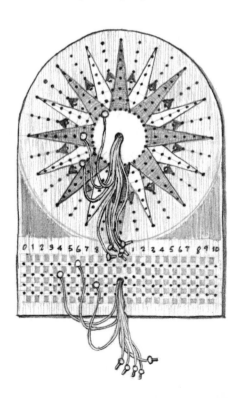

the first groove. If his estimated speed during the second half hour was six miles an hour, he placed the peg in the sixth hole of the second groove, and so on.

When the watch was over, the pilot could see from the traverse board what the course and rate of speed had been during the past four hours. He converted these peg markings into a summary of the course made good during the watch. At the end of the day he would "pick the chart" using a ruler and pair of compasses. A pair of compasses was an instrument with two pointed movable legs hinged at one end. It was used for taking measurements or drawing circles. The navigator placed one leg of the compass at the starting point on the chart. Positioning the ruler in the direction of the course steered, with the other end of the compass he pricked the distance made good. This was the new position of the ship.

Charts used at that time did not have lines of latitude and longitude. They had roses showing the compass directions and webs of lines extending from the compass directions and covering the chart. These lines were often drawn in different colors that matched the points on the ship's compass.

The navigator would determine the new course to steer by placing a ruler between the starting position and the destination. If the edge of the ruler coincided with a ray from the compass rose, this was the course to steer. If it did not coincide, the pair of compasses was opened out. As one point was moved along the ruler, a

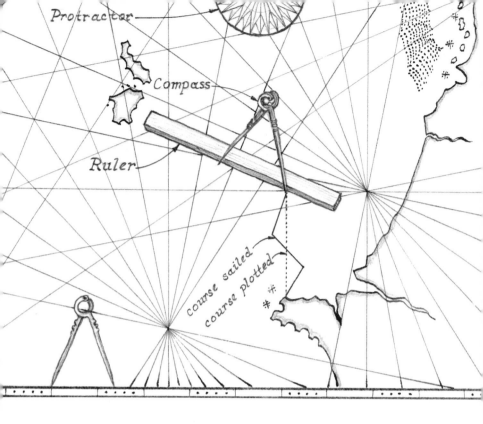

parallel ray was found with the other point. This was
then the course to steer.

This simple method served reasonably well, especially
in the days when few men could read or write. But
clearly there were many places for error. It is not sur-
prising that the crew would often see the officers argu-
ing about the exact position of the ship. Many variables
had to be accounted for, and many measurements relied on estimates. There were often errors in the original chart. The accuracy of each new position depended

on the accuracy of each starting point. Errors added up, and once a mistake was made, it was very difficult to find the true position again.

To keep the ships together as a fleet, general sailing orders were usually given before the voyage started. From then on, the ships did whatever the flagship did. This was fairly easy in daylight. They altered course when the flagship altered course and shortened sails when the flagship did. At night the ships tried to maintain equal speed and keep one another in sight by the light of the moon and the stars. They regrouped at dawn.

When visibility was poor, they had to have a system of signals. A lantern was fixed to the stern of the flagship. The lantern had an iron frame that housed two or three wax candles. Instead of glass, the candles were shielded by thin sheets of mica. The lantern gave a bright point of light that the other ships could follow through the darkness. The lantern was a sign of command; only the flagship could carry one.

To check that his fleet was behind him, the captain set another light beside the lantern. This was a signal for the other ships to show a single light. These signal lights were made by lighting a torch. The captain counted the lights to be sure the ships were following the flagship.

A simple code of torch signals was sometimes used to send orders. Each ship repeated the signal to show that the order was understood. Three lights might mean the crews should remove bonnets. Four lights might be used as a signal to lower sails. Fire was dangerous on wooden ships, especially with the wind blowing, so signals were kept to a minimum. If there was an emergency, sailors would light as many lights as possible and make as much noise as they could, shouting and firing weapons.

When complicated messages or orders had to be given, all sails were taken in and the ships would swing into the wind and hold there. Then the yawls were lowered and the captains rowed to the flagship. If the ships got separated, it was up to the others to find the flagship.

Life at Sea

For most of the journey, the lives of the sailors settled into a regular routine. The day was divided into four-hour parts called watches. The crew was divided into two groups. The groups took turns being on duty. The seamen on the watch did whatever work was necessary or stood by, ready to obey orders. When off watch, they were free to do what they wanted except for regular deck washing, church services, and emergencies. The afternoon and early evening watches may have been divided into two watches of two hours each. Then the crew would not always find themselves on the same watches; the two groups would alternate watches each day.

We know from the log that watches on Columbus's ships were set at three o'clock, seven o'clock, and eleven o'clock. Today, watches on ships are usually set at four, eight, and twelve o'clock. The watch from late at night until early in the morning is called the graveyard watch. It lasted from eleven P.M. to three A.M. on Columbus's ships and is the one all seamen find the most depressing. The men on the morning watch saw the new day begin. A ship's boy recited prayers to greet the dawn. The air felt fresh. The sails, the deck, and everything on the ship was damp with dew. The crew hauled up buckets of seawater and scrubbed the decks. The men inspected the ropes for places where they might be wearing thin. Usually they shifted ropes a little to keep one section of rope from getting the most strain. Seabirds sometimes joined the sailors on their journey, and dolphins appeared at times and played beside them. Sometimes there was good fishing and fresh food.

1st Day Watch   2nd Day Watch

At six-thirty the sand glass was turned for the seventh and last time that watch. The ship's boy would announce this with a special call:

Good is that which has past,
better that which shall come,
seven is past and eight floweth,
more shall flow if God wills,
count and pass makes voyage fast.

When the sands of the eighth glass had run out, the boy recited a call to the next watch, asking for God's protection for the watch to come. The men needed no time to dress; they slept in their clothes. They grabbed a biscuit, a bit of salted fish and some garlic cloves, or whatever was available for breakfast, and set to work. Before going off duty, the helmsman would give the course to the captain of the next watch. Lookouts were posted. The pilot transferred his reckoning from the traverse board to the chart and logbook. For most mariners, pumping ship was the first duty of every watch. Sometimes changing watches was called "summoning the men to pump." The off-going men grabbed something to eat and found a place to rest.

Meals were simple. The basic ration consisted of about one pound a day of hard biscuit with salted fish or meat, onion or garlic, and a ration of wine and water. The only hot meal of the day was served at about eleven

in the morning, the weather permitting. The sailors coming on duty could eat before going on watch, and the others could eat after they were relieved. Food was cooked on a stove set up on the deck. The stove was a three-sided iron box with a layer of sand and earth in the bottom. Firewood was burned on the sand, and the food was cooked in an iron pot hung from a bar. It was not an easy task to cook in the firebox with the ship rolling, the wind blowing, and waves splashing water on the deck. Wood for the fire was guarded as carefully as drinking water. Extra buckets of sand and seawater had to be kept nearby in case the deck caught fire. In heavy winds or storms no hot meals were prepared.

When they smelled food cooking, the crew lined up at the firebox. Each seaman carried his own plate or soup bowl, an eating knife, and a drinking horn for wine and water. The men extended their soup plates, then looked for a seat on the coils of rope or in the most protected place available. A boy walked around with a leather bottle and poured a small amount of wine for each man.

By three P.M. when the watch was set, the sailors had finished most of the day's work of scrubbing and making repairs. They could sit and talk, tell stories, tend a fishing line, wash themselves with buckets of salt water, or swim if the ocean was calm enough. During the early evening watch, all hands were called to say evening prayers and sing hymns. When the service ended, the boatswain made certain that the cooking fire was out.

The night watch was set, the helmsman was given his course, the lookouts were posted, and the ship sailed on into the night.

Life at sea was not comfortable. Meals rarely satisified hunger. Since food had to be stored for a long time in damp conditions, it was not long before most of the things to eat were rotten. Sometimes the men would save their biscuits to eat at night when they could not see the worms. Their thirst was never satisfied either. The water stored on board became so bad the men had to try to swallow it without looking, smelling, or tasting. And most of the food had been heavily salted to preserve it.

The places between decks lacked light and space. The toilet was over the gunwale, over the side of the ship. Rats, lice, cockroaches, and worms thrived in the damp, dark places below deck. There was a constant stench of bilge water, the water that collects in the bottom of the hold. Life on a ship was full of bad odors, filth, and discomfort. But life on land at that time was often hard and grim and not much better. At least in the middle of the sea, the air on deck was refreshing, and Columbus's crew had hopes of finding enough gold to make them all rich.

Many dangers could take them by surprise. Faith, luck, and regular routines were important to sailors living under such uncertain conditions. They liked to keep things they could control as certain as possible. They worried that changes might bring bad luck. The setting and rising of the sun were always marked by special prayers. Services were held on deck on Saturday and Sunday. Prayers were part of the everyday running of the ship. Many of the calls—for turning the sand glass, changing watches, relaying instructions, or the chants recited during long operations like winding in the anchor cable or hoisting a yard—were in part prayers. The rituals reminded the men that the safety of the ship depended as much on the grace of God as on their skill as mariners. In times of danger, sailors called upon God and saints, begging for protection and promising to worship and bring gifts to shrines if they survived.

The early days of the journey were smooth sailing, and the ships made good time. At night the sun went down ahead of them, and at dawn it came up behind them as they made their westward course. In the steady rhythm of the sea, they slipped farther and farther away from the known world.

Columbus kept two records of where they were and how far they had gone. One was what he believed was his true reckoning. This was for himself and for the King and Queen. The other was for the men sailing with him. On this accounting he gave shorter distances. He did not want the crew to become frightened at how far they were from the known world. More important, Columbus knew they would be frightened if land did not appear where he said it would be. They might want to turn back. His attempts to keep the crew from becoming alarmed were not very successful. The winds and currents were so favorable that many of the men feared that they would never be able to return to Spain. Finally he promised them he would turn back if the ships did not reach land in three days.

The Discovery

Everyone was on constant lookout for land and signs of land. Everyone wanted the long journey to be over, and the King and Queen had promised a reward of 10,000 maravedís a year for life to the man who first sighted land. There were several cries that were false alarms. At about ten P.M. on October 11, Columbus thought he spotted a small light like a candle. The ships continued sailing westward. At two A.M. the next morning, land was sighted by Rodrigo de Triana on the *Pinta*. Rodrigo was cheered and congratulated by his companions. Later, when it came to actually collecting the reward, Columbus challenged his claim on the basis of the light he had spotted earlier. The King and Queen accepted Columbus's word, and Columbus received the reward himself. Rodrigo de Triana was furious. According to some, he later hanged himself. Others say he converted to Islam and died fighting alongside the Moors. Some historians believe that Columbus could have seen a glow of torchlight from island people who fished and caught crabs at night. Most think he could not have seen anything at that distance; he just could not bear to have anyone but himself have the glory of first sighting land.

The fleet had left the Canary Islands on September 8, 1492, and they reached land on October 12. The actual ocean crossing took only thirty-three days. No one knows for certain the exact place of Columbus's first landfall. We know Columbus's dead reckoning of his position, but dead reckoning is not precise. Many investigators have tried to retrace Columbus's crossing and calculate his exact landfall. They have come up with many different theories, and they are all confident of their results. Watling Island, in the Bahamas, was the most widely agreed-upon spot. With the evidence of recent research, nearby Samana Cay is now gaining more acceptance as the place where the two worlds met.

Flags and banners were hoisted, and shields were hung from the sides of the ships. Columbus put on his scarlet doublet, and the officers dressed in their best clothes. Carrying the royal standard, they went ashore, claiming the island for Spain and naming it San Salvador. The people living there called their island Guanahani. The natives Columbus met were Arawak people of the Taino culture. Believing that he had reached the

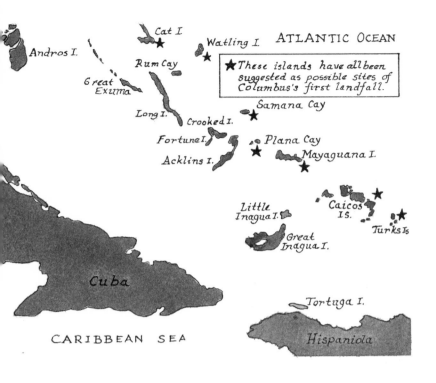

Indies, Columbus called the people Indians. This incorrect term was used by later explorers for all the many different native peoples of America. The native people greeted the strangers kindly, brought food and water, exchanged gifts, and seemed willing to share what they had. Columbus took some of the natives captive. He said that he did this so the Indians could learn about his people and give information to them. The information he wanted most was where to find gold.

Columbus had found land where he had expected to find it and concluded that he had reached an outlying

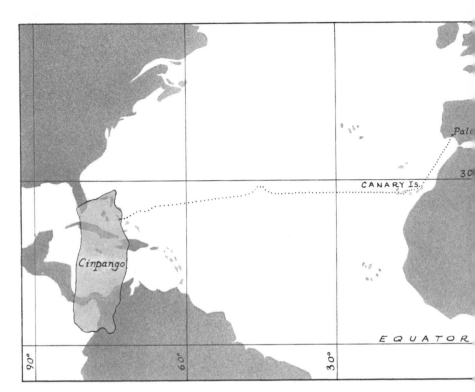

island of Asia. He sailed on, in search of Cipango, Cathay, and the Great Khan. His exploration of the islands
was the journey of a man trying to find his way in a
place he thought he should know. The islands were
lovely, the people were friendly, but something was
wrong. He expected to find great cities and great trading fleets. The native people seemed to know of gold
and pearls, but he could not find any. He could find
nothing that fit the descriptions of Japan and China.

Columbus's log is packed with vivid descriptions of
the lands he visited and their plant and animal life. His
writing shows his keen sensitivity to sights, sounds, and
fragrances. He described the people he encountered

and gave information about how they lived. He told about the Caribs, the cannibalistic enemies of the Taino people. The lands he explored were beautiful and full of interesting things. But he could not find the cities of gold and the fabulous wealth he had promised to bring back. There was nothing to prove that he had reached the outer limits of Asia.

Early in December Columbus arrived at what is now Haiti, which he named Española, and began exploring the coast. He came to a village where the young Arawak chief gave Columbus a belt with a beautiful gold mask on it as a gift. Columbus was eager to find more gold, and the natives mentioned Cibao, the name for the central part of Haiti. Columbus thought they were referring to Cipango. Before sunrise on December 24 he sailed off, hoping to spend Christmas in Japan.

By nightfall everyone was tired. The sea was calm. On the *Santa María* Columbus went to sleep, the master left the helmsman in charge, and the helmsman left the steering to a young ship's boy. This was against orders. Around midnight the ship went aground. The flagship was lost, but the men all made it to safety on the *Niña*. The next day, the chief who had given Columbus the gold mask had his people help the crew salvage everything they could from the wreckage. Columbus noted that not one thing was stolen from the ship by the natives who helped. There was not enough room on the other ships for all the men to return. They built a fort with help from the Indians, using timbers from the

Santa María. The settlement was called Navidad, which is the Spanish word for Christmas. Columbus had no trouble finding volunteers to stay behind. They all believed Cipango and vast quantities of gold were nearby. Columbus left supplies salvaged from the flagship.

The journey back to Spain was far more difficult than the outward voyage. The men faced terrible storms. Columbus finally returned to Palos on March 15, 1493. The voyage out, the exploration of the new lands, and

the voyage back took thirty-two weeks. They were thirty-two weeks that changed the history of mankind. Publications telling about his discovery were widely circulated through Spain and Europe. But at that time no one fully understood the significance of this journey. Everyone believed Columbus had reached Asia.

There was great excitement when Columbus traveled to present himself to the King and Queen at Barcelona. It was a fantastic procession; nothing quite like it had

ever been seen before. Columbus brought with him strange people — Indians from the other side of the world. Brightly colored parrots announced his approach with their screams. He carried strange plants and unknown spices and displayed unusual objects like the belt with a gold mask on it. Everything was new and exciting, and he was a sensation. People came out to see him all along the way. Towns and villages emptied and the roads were crowded with people wanting to see him and welcome him.

This was Columbus's greatest moment. He was received with honor by the King and Queen. He presented the original copy of the ship's log to the sovereigns. A coat of arms was bestowed on him. It had a gold castle on a green background in the upper left quarter. In the upper right corner was a purple lion with a green tongue on a white field. The lower left had gold islands in waves of the sea, and the lower right consisted of five gold anchors placed horizontally on a blue field. All of this was very important to Columbus. In those times, the opportunities to rise socially were extremely limited, and the difference between the life of a noble and that of a commoner was immense. Columbus was now Admiral of the Ocean Sea, and he became entitled to all the rights and privileges set down in the Capitulations. Preparations were rapidly being made for the second expedition to the Indies.

But Columbus's moment of glory was fleeting. The other three voyages proved disillusioning. When Co-

lumbus returned to the Indies, he found that all of the men he had left behind were dead, killed in confrontations with natives. Other attempts at colonies proved equally disastrous. The search for gold proved disappointing. He kept looking for Japan and China on all the voyages. It soon became certain that whatever he had found, it was not what he had promised. The crown was becoming less willing to invest in this venture that did not seem to be bringing the promised wealth to Spain.

The total cost of the Great Enterprise was about 2,000,000 maravedís. It is difficult to try to convert that into any meaningful modern terms. But during the era of discovery that followed, the court of Spain received 1,733,000 maravedís for every maravedí invested in financing Columbus's voyage. No matter how you figure it, it was one of the most profitable investments ever made.

Columbus died in Spain on May 20, 1506. He died believing he had reached Asia, although he certainly must have had some doubts. Mapmakers placed his discoveries as part of Asia, and it was many years before the idea was completely abandoned. At one time Columbus had been a national hero, but his death passed without much notice. He had hoped to gain power and wealth from his exploration, but he died powerless and poor.

He was buried in Spain, but sometime between 1541 and 1547 his remains were moved to Santo Domingo on the island he named Española and buried in the cathedral there. In 1795 when the French took over the island, what was believed to be his coffin was moved and buried in Havana, Cuba. When Spain lost control of Cuba in 1898, the coffin was returned to Spain and now rests in the cathedral of Seville. Like most things about Columbus, his place of burial is debated. There is disagreement as to whether it really was his remains that were in Cuba. In 1877 when the Santo Domingo cathedral was being repaired, a box was discovered with an inscription identifying the remains as those of Christopher Columbus. Today, at least three places claim to be where he is buried, and at least eight urns exist that are supposed to hold his ashes.

After Columbus had presented his log to the King and Queen, they'd had a copy made for him. Both the original and the copy are lost. Fortunately, before Columbus's copy disappeared, it passed through the hands of a Dominican friar, Bartolomé de Las Casas. He had seen Columbus's triumphant return to Spain when he was eighteen years old and was a great admirer of the explorer. Las Casas had been to the Indies, where he had been horrified by the treatment of the native people. He was writing a book called *History of the Indies* and had made a handwritten summary of the log to use in his work. Parts are quoted exactly, parts he omitted, and parts he edited, but the summary is generally regarded as an excellent synopsis of the original. Las Casas began compiling his history in 1527, but it was mostly written between 1550 and 1563. His book contains some things that are not in the log, and he knew personally many of the people who took part in the events of that time. The copy Las Casas made of the log lay forgotten in a library until it was discovered in 1790. It has since been translated into almost every language on earth. It is possible that the original log or the copy still remain in some forgotten collection somewhere.

Columbus's son, Ferdinand, wrote a biography of his father, whom he had accompanied on the fourth voyage. Ferdinand kept the annotated books his father had read; he had access to his father's copy of the log as well as all his personal papers.

Another writer living during that time was Fernández de Oviedo. Like Las Casas, he was also a young man when Columbus arrived triumphantly in Barcelona. Oviedo sailed to America in 1513 and spent thirty-four years in different parts of the West Indies. He wrote a book about the Indies in 1535. He had excellent powers of observation and was good at describing what he had seen and heard. Oviedo talked to many people who had known Columbus, and studied the documents and letters of the time.

Questions surround Columbus. Every detail about his life and accomplishments has been disputed and debated by scholars. We don't even know what he really looked like. We have descriptions from people who knew him, but all the portraits of him were made after his death. We think of Columbus as the man who discovered America, but we know he was not the first person to set foot on its soil. He found a land already inhabited by peoples of many different cultures. He was not even the first European in America. New evidence keeps suggesting earlier visits by Europeans.

Even his famous date of discovery is disputed. In 1492 the Christian world followed the Julian calendar. The Gregorian calendar we use today was adopted in 1582 by the Catholic world, and later by the English-speaking world. This means all Columbian dates must have nine days added to bring them in line with our current calendar. Columbus Day has not been corrected from the old-style dates; Columbus actually landed in America on October 21, 1492.

There is no doubt that the voyage of 1492 changed the world. He reached a land unknown to Europeans. He also discovered the two routes that are still considered the best ways to cross the Atlantic today. It took forty-five years after the first crossing to find a route across the Pacific Ocean. But even after five hundred years of experience navigating the Atlantic, seamen still travel the same routes that Columbus sailed. These ocean routes opened the way for further discoveries, but their importance was overshadowed by the lands being claimed and taken over.

Columbus's voyage began an era of exploration and discovery for the people of Europe. It also began an era of destruction and devastation for the native people of the land he claimed. When the Spaniards could not find enough gold and profitable cargo, they filled their ships with Indians to sell as slaves. They tried to force Indians to find gold for them. Indians were murdered, they committed suicide, and perished from diseases and overwork. Within two years after the arrival of Columbus and his men, one-half of the Taino people were dead. By 1515, only fifteen thousand were left, and by 1550 only five hundred. By 1650 the entire culture was gone. Spain and many other European countries gained wealth and power from the New World. They brought their cultures to the New World, but over and over again the same series of events would occur. Native tribes and cultures would be devastated in the confrontation with the Europeans.

Columbus has been given credit for the discovery of America, and he has been blamed for the disregard for native people and the destruction of the land. He has been called everything from a visionary and a prophet to a liar and a thief. His motives and his methods have been questioned. But his seamanship has rarely been disputed. Most experts consider Columbus a supreme sailor, the greatest dead-reckoning sailor who ever lived. The sea was Columbus's inspiration, and his real genius was as a seaman. It was Columbus who opened the Sea of Darkness to Europe and formed the connection between two land masses that were unknown to each other.

Bibliography

Anderson, R. C. *The Rigging of Ships*. Centreville, Maryland: Cornell Maritime Press, 1927. Reprinted 1984.

Anderson, Ruth Matilda. *Hispanic Costume, 1480–1530*. New York: Hispanic Society of America, 1979.

Bennett, J. A. *The Divided Circle: A History of Instruments for Astronomy, Navigation and Surveying*. Oxford, England: Phaidon–Christie's, 1987.

Bradford, Ernle. *Christopher Columbus*. New York: Viking, 1973.

Campbell, Tony. *The Earliest Printed Maps, 1472–1500*. Berkeley: University of California Press, 1987.

Cardini, Franco. *Europe 1492*. New York: Facts on File, 1989.

Connell, Evan S. *A Long Desire*. New York: Holt, Rinehart and Winston, 1979.

Cumming, W. P., R. A. Skelton, and D. B. Quinn. *The Discovery of North America*. New York: American Heritage Press, 1972.

Deagan, Kathleen A. "La Navidad, 1492: Searching for Columbus's Lost Colony." *National Geographic*, vol. 172, no. 5 (November 1987), pp. 672–675.

De Hevesy, André. *The Discoverer*. New York: Macaulay, 1928.

De Vorsey, Louis, Jr., and John Parker, eds. *In the Wake of Columbus: Islands and Controversy.* Detroit, Michigan: Wayne State University Press, 1985.

Fuson, Robert H. *The Log of Christopher Columbus.* Camden, Maine: International Marine Publishing Co., 1987.

Giardini, Cesare. *The Life and Times of Columbus.* Philadelphia: Curtis, 1966.

Gibson, Charles. *Spain in America.* New York: Harper & Row, 1966.

Granzotto, Gianni. *Christopher Columbus: The Dream and the Obsession.* Garden City, N.Y.: Doubleday, 1985.

Guye, Samuel, and Henri Michel. *Time and Space: Measuring Instruments from the 15th to the 19th Century.* New York: Praeger, 1971.

Jane, Cecil. *The Journal of Christopher Columbus.* New York: Bramhall House, 1960.

Judge, Joseph. "Where Columbus Found the New World." *National Geographic,* vol. 170, no. 5 (November 1986), pp. 566–599.

Landström, Björn. *Columbus.* New York: Macmillan, 1966.

Lyon, Eugene. "15th-Century Manuscript Yields First Look at *Niña.*" *National Geographic,* vol. 170, no. 5 (November 1986), pp. 600–605.

McKee, Alexander. *How We Found the "Mary Rose."* New York: St. Martin's Press, 1982.

Mahn-Lot, Marianne. *Columbus.* New York: Grove Press, 1961.

Marden, Luis. "The First Landfall of Columbus." *National Geographic,* vol. 170, no. 5 (November 1986), pp. 572–577.

Mariéjol, Jean Hippolyte. *The Spain of Ferdinand and Isabella.* New Brunswick, N.J.: Rutgers University Press, 1961.

Martinez-Hidalgo, José María. *Columbus' Ships.* Barre, Vt.: Barre Publishers, 1966.

Morison, Samuel Eliot. *Admiral of the Ocean Sea: A Life of Christopher Columbus* (2 vols.). Boston: Little, Brown, 1942.

———. *The European Discovery of America: The Northern Voyages,* A.D. *500–1600.* New York: Oxford University Press, 1971.

———. *The European Discovery of America: The Southern Voyages,* A.D. *1492–1616.* New York: Oxford University Press, 1974.

Nance, R. Morton. "Caravels." *The Mariner's Mirror,* vol. 3, no. 9 (September 1913), pp. 265–271.

Nunn, George E. *The Geographical Conceptions of Columbus.* New York: American Geographical Society, 1924.

Parry, J. H. *The Discovery of the Sea.* New York: Dial Press, 1974.

Penrose, Boies. *Travel and Discovery in the Renaissance, 1420–1620.* Cambridge, Mass.: Harvard University Press, 1952.

"Report on the *Santa María* of Columbus." *The Mariner's Mirror,* vol. 16, no. 2 (April 1930), pp. 187–195.

Roberts, Gail, ed. *Atlas of Discovery.* New York: Gallery Books, 1989.

Sanz, Carlos. *El mapa del mundo.* Madrid: La real sociedad geográphica, 1966.

"Shipshape: Rebuilding Columbus' Famous Trio for a 1992 Voyage to the New World." *Life,* April 1989, pp. 26–30.

Singer, Charles, E. J. Holmyard, A. R. Hall, and Trevor I. Williams, eds. *A History of Technology,* vols. 2 and 3. Oxford, England: Oxford University Press, 1957.

Skelton, R. A. *Explorers' Maps.* London: Routledge and Kegan Paul, 1958.

Stevenson, Edward Luther, ed. *Atlas of Portolan Charts.* New York: Hispanic Society of America, 1911.

Svensson, Sam. *Sails Through the Centuries.* New York: Macmillan, 1965.

Taviani, Paolo Emilio. *Christopher Columbus: The Grand Design.* London: Orbis Publications, 1985.

Taylor, Eva Germaine Rimington. *The Haven-Finding Art.* London: Hollis & Carter, 1956.

Thacher, John Boyd. *Christopher Columbus: His Life, His Work, His Remains* (3 vols.). New York, 1903.

Tooley, R. V., and Charles Bricker. *Landmarks of Mapmaking.* New York: Dorset Press, 1989.

Vietor, Alexander O. "A Pre-Columbian Map of the World, circa 1489." *Yale University Library Gazette,* vol. 37, no. 1 (July 1962), pp. 8–12.

Wilford, John Noble. "Dominican Bluff Yields Columbus's First Colony." *New York Times,* November 27, 1990, pp. C1 and C6.

———. *The Mapmakers.* New York: Vintage, 1982.

Zinn, Howard. *A People's History of the United States.* New York: Harper & Row, 1980.

Books for Children

For Further Reading

Berger, Josef. *Discoverers of the New World*. New York: American Heritage, 1960.

Brownlee, Walter. *The First Ships Round the World*. New York: Cambridge University Press, 1974.

Cairns, Trevor. *Europe Finds the World*. New York: Cambridge University Press, 1973.

Ceserani, Gian Paolo. *Marco Polo*. New York: G. P. Putnam's Sons, 1982.

Dolan, Sean J. *Christopher Columbus: The Intrepid Mariner*. New York: Ballantine Books, 1989.

Finkelstein, Norman H. *The Other 1492*. New York: Charles Scribner's Sons, 1989.

Fritz, Jean. *Brendan the Navigator: A History Mystery about the Discovery of America*. New York: Coward, McCann and Geoghegan, 1979.

————. *Where Do You Think You're Going, Christopher Columbus?* New York: G. P. Putnam's Sons, 1980.

Fuson, Robert H. *The Log of Christopher Columbus*. Camden, Maine: International Marine Publishing Co., 1987.

Humble, Richard. *The Age of Leif Eriksson.* New York: Franklin Watts, 1989.

Irwin, Constance. *Strange Footprints on the Land: Vikings in America.* New York: Harper and Row, 1980.

Krensky, Stephen. *Who Really Discovered America?* New York: Scholastic Inc., 1987.

Las Casas. *The Log of Christopher Columbus' First Voyage to America.* New York: William R. Scott, 1938. (and Hamden, Conn.: The Shoestring Press, 1989).

Levinson, Nancy Smiler. *Christopher Columbus, Voyager to the Unknown.* New York: Lodestar Dutton, 1990.

McKendrick, Melveena. *Ferdinand and Isabella.* New York: American Heritage, 1968.

Meltzer, Milton. *Columbus and the World Around Him.* New York: Franklin Watts, 1990.

Osborne, Mary Pope. *The Story of Christopher Columbus, Admiral of the Ocean Sea.* New York: Dell Publishing Co., 1987.

Poole, Frederick King. *Early Exploration of North America.* New York: Franklin Watts, 1989.

Roop, Peter and Connie Roop, eds. *I, Columbus: My Journal 1492–3.* New York: Walker and Co., 1990.

Rugoff, Milton. *Marco Polo's Adventures in China.* New York: American Heritage, 1964.

Ventura, Piero. *Christopher Columbus.* New York: Random House, 1978.

Wilbur, C. Keith. *Early Explorers of North America.* Chester, Connecticut: Globe Pequot Press, 1989.

Index